The Family Blessing

THE FAMILY BLESSING

Rolf Garborg

WORD PUBLISHING
Dallas·London·Vancouver·Melbourne

The Family Blessing
Copyright © 1990 by Rolf Garborg

Unless otherwise specified, all Scripture quotations are from *The Everyday Bible, New Century Version,* copyright © 1987, 1988 by Word Publishing, Dallas, Texas 75039. Used by permission. Other Scripture quotations are from the following sources: The Authorized King James Version (KJV), The New King James Version (NKJV), copyright © 1979 by Thomas Nelson, Inc., Publishers. The New American Standard Bible (NASB), © the Lockman Foundation 1960, 1962, 1963, 1968, 1971, 1972, 1973, 1975, 1977. The New International Version of the Bible (NIV), copyright © 1978 by the New York International Bible Society. Used by permission of Zondervan Bible Publishers.

If you would like more information regarding *The Family Blessing,* please contact:
Rolf Garborg
Box 31153
Bloomington, Minnesota 55431

Library of Congress Cataloging in Publication Data

Garborg, Rolf, 1943–
    The family blessing / by Rolf Garborg, foreword by Gary Smalley and John Trent.
        p.   cm.
    ISBN 0-8499-0781-0
    1. Family—Religious life.   2. Benediction.   I. Title.
BV4526.2.G37   1990
249—dc20   90-35770
                                                                      CIP

Printed in the United States of America
0 1 2 3 4 9 RRD 9 8 7 6 5 4 3 2 1

To Mary, my precious wife of twenty-two years, my most ardent friend, encourager, counselor, and companion, and mother of my two most cherished gifts from God, Carlton and Lisa.

Acknowledgments

Grateful thanks are in order to many friends who have had a part in bringing this book to life:

• Mary, my wife, for her constant encouragement and participation through the past eighteen years of blessing our children. Also, for her patience in reading the longhand manuscript of this book and putting it all on computer. Thank you, Mary!

• Carlton and Lisa, the two gifts of love God has given Mary and me. Knowing that Dad was going to tell more about them than they cared to have told, they gave me nothing but encouragement as I wrote. Without their heartfelt consent, I would not have proceeded. Thank you both from the bottom of my heart.

• Paul Thigpen, the incredibly talented editor God dropped in my lap. Paul's skills as a writer and editor are great, but it was his life and spirit that touched me most. Thank you, Paul.

• Byron Williamson at Word who believed in this book enough to pursue it for two years. Without his encouragement and interest it likely would not exist. Thank you, Byron, for your friendship and trust in me.

• Christine Scott, Ken and Loretta Wittig, Lonnie Hull, Susan Heuser, Lee Gessner, Ben Haden, Larry Christenson, Gary Smalley and John Trent, Dan and Joy Straley, Gary and Carol Johnson, Bill and Karen Hulten, my family and others who prodded and urged me to pursue this project. I am grateful to you all and thank you.

Contents

◇

Foreword

"Please bless me, even me also, Oh my father . . ." Genesis 27:34

Haunting words. Words spoken by Esau when his father's blessing slipped out of his hands forever . . . and words echoed by thousands of modern-day Esau's who have also missed out on the greatest earthly gift their parents could have given them.

For years, we've seen men and women struggle with the very real problem of missing out on their parents' "blessing." From emotional pain to unhealthy procrastination, from substance abuse to an inability to maintain intimate relationships, missing this important gift from a parent can affect some people for a lifetime.

What is this "blessing" that was so important in Old Testament times, and still remains so vital to a child's emotional and spiritual life today? That question led us to write a book about this important concept, and now to recommend this important book that you hold in your hands.

In Rolf Garborg's book, *The Family Blessing,* you'll discover the very personal story about how one family put into practice the elements of the Old Testament "Blessing" to enrich their family—and many others as well. What's more, you'll see how making a regular time of "blessing" a part of your parenting style can strengthen your family relationships dramatically.

But why is it so important to learn to "bless" our children?

We recently heard the story of a father who took his teenage son with him to a small, private airport. It was a warm summer afternoon, and they were going to meet a close family friend who was an experienced stunt pilot.

As the son stood and watched, the father climbed into his friend's two-seater plane. Soon they were airborne, doing aerobatic stunts that the veteran pilot had practiced safely for years. As the plane came out of a steep dive, it suddenly stalled, and then something went terribly wrong with its controls. In a moment's time, the plane tumbled out of the sky and crashed near the runway.

The first one to reach the plane was this man's son. The teenager pulled the pilot from the wreckage first, and though in pain, it was obvious that he would live. But as he pulled his father out of the wreckage, it was even more obvious that he would not.

In all, some forty minutes passed before an ambulance came from the small town nearby. Yet during that agonizing wait, something miraculous happened. In the space of a few minutes, a father was able to clearly communicate and give his son his "blessing," and a son was able to return it to his father as well.

This man died when he was only a few miles from the hospital—but his words and actions of blessing that day will stay with his son all his life.

Most of us have years, not minutes to live. If anything, the everyday routines we set up tend to push aside any urgency we may feel to communicate our blessing to our children. However, none of us knows the day, nor the hour, and we share this touching story to ask a question:

"If you had forty minutes to live, would you know for a fact that you could clearly communicate the 'blessing' to your children?" You could if you were this man, and you'll be able to after reading this book.

We have taught, written, counseled, and consistently practiced with our own family members the powerful principles that surround this Old Testament practice. In short, we're 100 percent behind this concept and in support of this book. In the pages that follow, you'll find many practical "how tos" when it comes to communicating this "blessing" to your family. You'll also be touched, challenged, instructed, and encouraged to make a daily gift of unconditional love to all those you wish to bless.

Gary Smalley and John Trent, Ph.D.

---◇---

Introduction

A. W. Tozer once said, "If it's good, God did it. And if it's bad, I did it, and it's worse than it looks."

As I reflect on my life, and especially on the past eighteen years that my wife Mary and I have been blessing our children, Tozer's statement rings incredibly true. It seems as if every time I began to look admiringly at something I had done well and to take credit for it, God would allow something to happen that would straighten out my thinking.

Sometimes He would let me fall down; other times I would have to be knocked down. Sometimes correction would come through direct confrontation from a friend honest enough to tell me the truth about myself; sometimes a subtle, sarcastic remark from an acquaintance would do the job. And sometimes it was just the hollow emptiness that came when I took credit for something I knew I didn't deserve.

The family blessing is a clear example of Tozer's principle. I know that the practice of blessing the family is good, and a gift from God. But more than that, I know that even though *we* pronounce the blessing, *God* is the one who actually blesses. We are just the instruments He uses, the vessels through whom He flows. And because God's gifts are meant to be shared rather than hoarded, I'm offering this book.

In no way do I mean to communicate that all has gone smoothly either in my life or in the lives of my wife and children. We have had our share of failures, setbacks, problems, and disappointments—just as you probably have. Only God's grace has made it work, and I'm grateful that He is still at work in us.

His grace is at work in your home, too, and He'll be faithful to help you learn ways to bless your family.

When I first read in Larry Christenson's book, *The Christian Family*, about his experiences of blessing his children, I thought, *I want to know more about this*. The story of that discovery is told in the chapters that follow. I'm eternally grateful for the insight Larry gave me into this practice, and I pray that you'll feel the same as you read on.

During the past eighteen years, I've shared our practice of blessing our children with a number of other families. Their responses have almost always been the same. They've usually said:

1. "I wish I had known this when my kids were young."
2. "I wish my parents had done that for me." (This comment came mostly from teen-agers.)
3. "How do I get started doing it myself?"
4. "What blessings do you use, and where do you find them?"
5. "Why don't you write a book about this?"

Here's the book they asked for. It will help you learn about the family blessing and how to get started doing it yourself. It will suggest some blessings to use. And it will offer some insights into what the family blessing can mean to you even if you never received it as a child yourself, and even if your children are already out of the nest. It's never too late to bless and be blessed.

I sincerely pray that you will hear and heed what God has to say to you through this book. God bless you as you read!

I

◇

The Family Blessing

> *The Lord bless you, and keep you;*
> *The Lord make His face shine on you*
> *And be gracious to you;*
> *The Lord lift up His countenance on you,*
> *And give you peace.*
>
> Numbers 6:24–26, NASB

1

◇

How Our Family Came to Know the Blessing

I still remember the scene vividly: It was a balmy January evening in San Juan, Puerto Rico, eighteen years ago. The nighttime street noises came freely through the open louvered window of the bedroom as my young son, Carlton, lay sound asleep.

I don't remember how long I simply stood by his bed that night, thinking about what a treasure he was to us. So many times before Carlton was born I had watched other fathers with their young children perched on their shoulders or walking hand-in-hand with them, and I had looked forward to that day myself. Now that I had a son of my own who was nearly three years old, I wanted so desperately to be a good father to him.

Carlton didn't even stir when I sat on the edge of his bed. As I leaned over his little body, I thought, *Lord Jesus, You showed us how much You care for these little ones when You took them in Your arms and blessed them. Now I want to do the same for my child. Take this blessing of mine and use it for Your glory.* Then I placed my hand gently on his head and whispered into his ear a blessing I had heard so many times in church, adding to it his name:

The Lord bless you, Carlton, and keep you.
The Lord make His face shine upon you and be
    gracious unto you;

*The Lord lift up His countenance upon you and give
you peace.
In the name of the Father, and of the Son, and of the
Holy Spirit. Amen.*

It seemed so natural—so right. I felt as if I had obeyed God in the act.

Before I rose to leave Carlton's room, I kissed him on the cheek, told him I loved him, and wiped the remaining tears from my face. Then I lingered there in the darkness and breathed a prayer of thanks to God for giving us this gift of a son, and for blessing him. Little did I realize that the scene would be repeated thousands of times in the years to come.

How It All Began

That was the first night I ever gave my son a blessing. The idea was new to me at the time, and I didn't fully understand what it was all about. But after talking with another Christian father who gave his children a blessing every night, I had become convinced that this simple practice could transform our children's lives.

It all began in 1972 when my wife, Mary, and I were on the mission field in Puerto Rico, where I served as Director of Bethany Literature Fellowship. It was a literature mission in San Juan with a bookstore, a fledgling Spanish publishing house, and a fleet of energetic young Christians who were going door-to-door with their testimony of salvation and a satchel of books from our store.

That year a recently released bestseller caught my eye: *The Christian Family,* by Larry Christenson.[1] In it the author, who at the time was the pastor of a Lutheran church in San Pedro, California, clearly and biblically showed us God's order for the family and how we can practice the presence of Jesus in the home. I was immediately taken by the simplicity of the message in this book and began to recommend it to others.

When an opportunity came to invite Larry to Puerto Rico, I gladly took advantage of it. He agreed to come spend a week at our mission, teaching and sharing with us both individually and as a group.

One evening when Larry, Mary, and I were having an evening snack, I asked him about one particular point in his book that had aroused my curiosity. The final section in his chapter "The Priesthood of Parents" was called "Presenting Your Children to God—Through Blessing." It dealt with the Christensons' practice of speaking a blessing on their children individually as they put them to bed each night, and I wanted to know more about it.

Larry was only too happy to tell us more. He said that he and his wife, Nordis, had been living in West Germany with their four young children when they first heard of the idea in 1959. They had learned about the custom from a German couple they had met, Hans-Jochen Arp and his wife, Elisabeth.

One evening Hans-Jochen told them, almost in passing, how he would speak a blessing on each of his six children as they went to bed. Even if they were already asleep when he came home late, he would go into their bedrooms and bless them.

Larry and Nordis were so impressed with the idea of a family blessing that they went home that very night to bless their own children. First, they explained to them what they were doing and why. With four children, it took awhile to give everyone an individual blessing. But they did it and they continued to do it faithfully, night after night, year after year, until each child had grown up and left home. Now, a dozen years later, Larry was passing the idea on to others.

Parents Are the Priests of Their Homes

The idea Larry proposed made good sense to us. After all, we knew that many pastors do the very same thing to their congregations at the end of each Sunday church service. Often they hold out their hands toward the people in a symbolic gesture of covering and then recite a benediction from the words of

Scripture, such as the one the high priest Aaron spoke over the ancient Israelites:

> The Lord bless you and keep you;
> the Lord make His face shine upon you and be
>   gracious unto you;
> the Lord lift His countenance upon you, and give you
>   peace
>
> Numbers 6:24–26[2]

Then they may add words such as these: "In the name of the Father, and of the Son, and of the Holy Spirit. Amen."

Just as the pastor of a congregation has an opportunity to bless them, we realized that parents as priests in their own households have a similar privilege. They can speak at home the kind of blessing pastors speak to their churches.

As we talked with Larry on into the night, I became convinced that this family practice was right for us as well. I didn't realize back then how many benefits could come from making this commitment to bless my children. But I knew I wanted to do it, and I wanted to begin right away.

So then and there I made a decision. Whenever and however possible, I would bless my child every day. And I would begin right away.

A Prenatal Blessing

After I'd given Carlton a blessing that evening, Mary and I talked over what had happened and agreed together to commit to this practice every night as we tucked him into bed. I told her I could hardly wait for the next night to come so I could do it again, this time with Carlton awake.

Meanwhile, Mary was just three months away from giving birth to our second child. We didn't know whether it was a boy or a girl, but it really didn't matter. We would welcome either, or one of each for that matter.

During our discussion I had already begun thinking of how it would be to have two kids to bless when we tucked them in each night. But then as we continued talking the realization came to me: We weren't done with the blessing this evening yet. I already *had* two children. Why not start now to bless them both? So I reached out my hand, placed it on Mary's tummy, and said, "Lord, I don't have any idea who it is you have for us in here, but I commit this gift of a child to you." Then, speaking to that unborn baby with my hand still on its mother's tummy, I said, "The Lord bless you, precious child, and keep you . . ." and I spoke the rest of the blessing, just as I had with Carlton.

On April 23, 1972, Lisa Faith Garborg entered this world "sunny side up," and she hasn't quit smiling yet. No doubt one reason for her joy is that she has been blessed every day by her fathers—both earthly and heavenly—since even before she was born.

Carlton and Lisa are now twenty-one and eighteen years old respectively, and amazingly enough, both Carlton and Lisa still call home every day—not just to check up on Mom and Dad, but also to receive their daily blessing. (You can imagine how grateful I am that their schools are local so they don't have to call collect!)

My children's desire to continue having our blessing every day is just one indication of the impact it has made on their lives. Just how great that impact has been, I may never fully know. But this much is clear: The family blessing is much more than a bedtime ritual. As we take a look now at the significance of the blessing from a biblical standpoint, we'll begin to discover why it can become such a meaningful part of the fabric of daily family life.

Blessed shall you be in the city, and blessed shall you be in the country.
Blessed shall be the offspring of your body and the produce of your ground and the offspring of your beasts, the increase of your herd and the young of your flock.
Blessed shall be your basket and your kneading bowl.
Blessed shall you be when you come in, and blessed shall you be when you go out.

Deuteronomy 28:3–6, NASB

2

◇

The Biblical Blessing

When God launched Abraham onto a course that would fulfill his unique destiny, He had to send him out of his parents' home into a challenging adventure in unknown territory. No doubt Abraham's excitement over his future was mixed with considerable apprehension over what might lie ahead—the same kind of apprehension most of us felt when we first launched out on our own, leaving our parents' home forever.

How did God choose to prepare Abraham for the days ahead and to encourage him along the way? He sent him out with a *blessing*. God said:

> I will make you into a great nation and I will bless
>   you;
> I will make your name great, and you will be a
>   blessing.
> I will bless those who bless you, and whoever curses
>   you I will curse;
> and all peoples on earth will be blessed through you.
> Genesis 12:2–3, NIV

With these words the Lord spoke to Abraham a blessing of greatness, promised further blessing in the future, and said He would make the man a blessing to others—even a channel of blessing to the entire world. No doubt in the years to come, whenever Abraham faced tough times in life, these words from God strengthened and sustained him.

Throughout the biblical record we find ample evidence that the God of Abraham was a God of blessing—in fact, the words "bless" or "blessing" appear in Scripture in some form or another about seven hundred times. Apparently both Abraham and countless other people in the Bible as well needed and welcomed the grace, power, and encouragement that could be poured into their lives through God's blessing.

But what exactly is a blessing? The word has a variety of meanings in modern English, so we need to look at two ancient biblical words that can help us define what we're talking about.

Common Notions of "Blessing"

When my friend Dan told his mother that a friend of his was writing a book, she was excited. She asked Dan what the book was about, and he told her it was about our practice of blessing our kids when we put them to bed. "Well, Dan," she noted with a measure of pride, "we blessed you, too, when you were a child."

Dan looked at her rather quizzically and wondered out loud, "You did? When did you do that?"

"Well," she confessed, "it was usually when you sneezed, but we *did* bless you."

Dan was still laughing about the conversation when he called me several days later. His mother had been absolutely sincere, but she had had in mind a notion of what it means to bless children that was completely different than ours. No doubt in millions of homes today the only blessing given at all to the children is a well-intentioned "God bless you" after a sneeze. Yet even then the significance of the words has been lost by the secularizing force of familiarity.

In fact, today Christians have often overused the word "blessing" to the point that they've almost emptied the word of any meaning at all. But the biblical significance of the term is of profound importance to our daily lives.

Blessings Convey God's Power

The Old Testament Hebrew word for blessing is *berakah*. To the ancient Hebrews, a *berakah* was the *transmittal or endowment of the power of God's goodness and favor,* usually through the spoken word and often with the accompanying act of the laying on of hands.[1] For Abraham, the *berakah* was God's spoken declaration of favor that would convey God's power to make him into a great nation able to transmit that divine favor and power to the whole world.

The Hebrews believed that the spoken word carried with it great power for good or evil. In fact, most ancient peoples were convinced, as the Hebrews were, that words—once spoken— had a life of their own. So when a word of blessing was given, the speaker could not retract it.

That was the case with Isaac's blessing, which was given mistakenly to his younger son, Jacob, rather than to his first-born, Esau (see Genesis 27:1–40). In this Bible story we read that Jacob tricked his blind father into thinking he was Esau, so that Isaac placed his hands on Jacob and pronounced on him the blessing of the firstborn child that rightfully belonged to Esau. Once Isaac spoke the words, there was nothing he could do to take back the blessing, even though it had been gained by deceit. The most the saddened father could do was to speak another blessing on Esau.

Benedictions (that is, spoken blessings) such as Isaac's were commonly spoken by fathers to their children. They were also given by people in authority to those under their authority, or by priests to the congregation of believers. Such benedictions always included the name of God.

Blessings "Speak Well of" Someone

In the New Testament the word most often translated as "bless" is the Greek verb *eulogeo,* from which we get the words "eulogy" and "eulogize." It means literally "to speak well of" or "to express praise."

As in the Old Testament, this kind of blessing was most often the act of calling down God's gracious power on someone. One clear example we have of this act in the New Testament is Jesus' blessing on the disciples just before He ascended to heaven, when He promised that God would send the gracious power of the Holy Spirit on them (see Luke 24:48–51).

Four Types of Blessing

One useful way to think about blessings for our present purposes is to distinguish them according to who is giving the blessing and who or what is receiving the blessing. Using these criteria, we find four types of blessing in the Scripture.

The first type is a benediction *spoken by God to people,* promising His favor. The blessing of Abraham was of this kind.

The second type is a blessing *spoken by people to God.* When we "speak well" or "express praise" to God, then we're blessing Him, as David said: "*Bless* the Lord, O my soul, and forget none of His benefits" (Psalm 103:2, NASB). The apostle Paul echoed that sentiment when he wrote to the Ephesians, "*Blessed* be the God and Father of our Lord Jesus Christ, who has *blessed* us with every spiritual *blessing* . . ." (Ephesians 1:3, NKJV).

The third type of blessing is *spoken by God or people over things.* The twenty-eighth chapter of Deuteronomy is filled with this kind of blessing; there God promises to pour out His favor on the material resources of the Israelites if they obey Him: "*Blessed* shall be . . . the produce of your ground and the offspring of your beasts . . . *Blessed* shall be your basket and your kneading bowl" (Deuteronomy 28:4–5, NASB).

People also spoke blessings over things as a way of dedicating them to God and setting them apart for His favor. The most common example of this kind of benediction is the blessing of food, an ancient Jewish custom that continued in the Christian community. Jesus showed the great potential power of such a practice when He blessed the loaves and fishes, calling down God's miraculous power to multiply them (Matthew 14:19–21).

The fourth type of blessing is the blessing *spoken by one person to another,* often in the name of God, who is of course the ultimate source of all blessing. Isaac's blessing of Jacob is one example of this kind; Aaron's blessing on the Israelites (quoted in the previous chapter) is another.

Two Meanings

Within this last category of blessing—which will receive our primary attention in this book—we should note that the word can have both a general meaning and a more specific one. The general meaning is best kept in mind by the literal translation of *eulogeo:* "to speak well of, to express praise."

This is the sense probably intended when Jesus told His disciples, "*Bless* those who curse you, pray for those who mistreat you" (Luke 6:28, NIV). Thus Paul was obeying the Lord's command when he replied to his persecutors with gracious speech: "When we are cursed," he told the Romans, "we bless . . . when we are slandered, we answer kindly" (Romans 4:12–13, NIV).

The more specific meaning of blessing is the intentional act of speaking God's favor and power into someone's life, often accompanied by a symbolic gesture such as laying hands on the person. This is the kind of blessing spoken by Isaac to his son Jacob, and in turn by Jacob to his sons (Genesis 48:8–49:28). It's the type of blessing Jesus gave to His disciples (Luke 24:50) and to the children (Mark 10:16).

To learn about the special power and promise of the family blessing—which is the focus of this book—we need to look at both the specific and the general meanings of blessing within the context of family life. When we recognize the power of the spoken word for good or evil in our daily interactions with those at home, we can learn to use that power intentionally to bring blessing to our children.

In chapter eight we'll consider what it might mean to bless our children by "speaking well" of them from day to day. But next we'll look at the family blessing as an intentional act of speaking God's favor and power into our children's lives.

How blessed is everyone who fears the Lord,
Who walks in His ways.
When you shall eat of the fruit of your hands,
You will be happy and it will be well with you.
Your wife shall be like a fruitful vine,
Within your house,
Your children like olive plants
Around your table.
Behold, for thus shall the man be blessed
Who fears the Lord.
The Lord bless you,
And may you see prosperity all the days of your life.
Indeed, may you see your children's children!
Peace be upon God's people!

adapted from Psalm 128, NASB

3

◇

What Is the Family Blessing?

The hit musical play and film *Fiddler on the Roof* has tugged at the heartstrings of thousands of parents with its charming story of love and conflict in family life. Many of us fathers and mothers can well identify with the hopes and fears, the convictions and questions of Jewish Papa Tevye and Mama Golde as they struggle to rear their children in a godly way and to help them prepare for a happy and productive adult life.

One of the most poignant scenes from the play shows the Jewish family at the table of the Sabbath meal. When all have gathered, they carry out the ancient customs associated with that meal in which they have participated every week of their lives. The mother lights the Sabbath candles, prays, and then joins her husband in singing to the children (all daughters) "Sabbath Prayer," a simple song of blessing that sums up their desires for them:

> *May the Lord protect and defend you,*
> *May He always shield you from shame;*
> *May you come to be in Yisroel [Israel] a shining*
>   *name.*
> *May you be like Ruth and like Esther,*
> *May you be deserving of praise;*
> *Strengthen them, oh Lord, and keep them from the*
>   *stranger's ways.*
> *May God bless you and grant you long lives,*
> *May the Lord fulfill our Sabbath prayer for you.*

> *May God make you good mothers and wives.*
> *May He send you husbands who will care for you.*
> *May the Lord protect and defend you,*
> *May the Lord preserve you from pain;*
> *Favor them, oh Lord, with happiness and peace,*
> *Oh hear our Sabbath prayer. Amen.* [1]

What Christian father or mother doesn't hear echoed in those words the deepest sentiments of his or her own heart? And yet how many of us have a regular setting, as the family in the play did, where such powerful words can be expressed to our children?

Christian families don't have to envy the Jewish community's ancient tradition of parents' giving their children a benediction. We need only adopt this biblical custom ourselves, personalizing it according to our family's individual needs.

We may say a blessing or sing it; give it daily or weekly or just on special occasions; recite one from the Scripture or create our own. But however we choose to bless our children, the family blessing—acted out so beautifully on the stage in this play—can become a real-life scene in our own homes. And it will confirm our children in godliness by speaking into their lives the grace of their heavenly Father.

Our Children's Highest Good

When Jesus came to earth two thousand years ago, He came with one overwhelming task to accomplish. That task was to give Himself to our highest good, that we would know and love God with all our heart. Just read what He prayed to His Father in John 17:3–4: "And this is eternal life: that men can know you, the only true God, and that men can know Jesus Christ, the One you sent. I finished the work you gave me to do. I brought you glory on earth."

Again in Luke 10:25–28, when Jesus was questioned by a teacher of the law on how to gain eternal life, He replied with a question: "What is written in the law?" The teacher answered, "Love the Lord your God. Love him with all your heart, all your soul, all your strength, and all your mind. And you must love your neighbor as you love yourself." Then Jesus said to him, "Your answer is right. Do this and you will have life forever."

I believe that the single most important concern for us as parents should be the same primary concern Jesus has for us: *We must make it our ultimate goal to help our children know and love God with all they are.*

How can we do that? Numerous books and articles have been written to answer this question, presenting useful guidelines and insights for almost every area of parenting. But I am convinced that one of the simplest and most powerful ways to help our children know and love God is to *give them a daily, concrete encounter with His power and favor through laying hands on them and speaking a blessing on them.*

The Parent's Blessing

The notion of a parent speaking a blessing on a child may seem novel to many families, but it's actually an ancient and respected custom dating back to biblical times. In fact, the family setting for the blessing apparently predates its use in the public setting; the priest or other official who spoke benedictions on the people of Israel was only supplementing the most basic of blessings —the one given by the father to the children.

Even those of us who have never given or received this kind of blessing have probably caught glimpses of it in various contexts. Benedictions in church services are one example; the scene just described in *Fiddler on the Roof* is another. Several Old Testament stories also focus on this custom, some of which we have already mentioned: Isaac's blessing of Jacob (Genesis 27); Jacob's blessing of his sons and grandsons (Genesis 48:8–49:33); the priest Melchizedek's blessing of Abram (Genesis 14:18–20); the high priest Aaron's blessing of the Israelites (Numbers 6:23–27); and the prophet Balaam's blessing of the Israelites (Numbers 23:7–24:9).

How We Use the Blessing in Our Home

The way we approached the family blessing in our home was quite simple. We basically repeated what I did with Carlton that first evening I blessed him in San Juan, except we did it when the kids were awake.

Each night at bedtime, I would lay my hands on the head of each of my children and speak to them the blessing that appears in Numbers 6:24–26, adding at the end the words "in the name of the Father, and of the Son, and of the Holy Spirit." I also would personalize the blessing by adding the child's name at the end of the first phrase: "The Lord bless you and keep you, Lisa. . . ."

It was as simple as that. We had no need to make long and involved speeches, nor to keep coming up with different blessings for the sake of novelty. We just spoke the same blessing, night after night, to each of our children. And they came to depend upon it as a token of security and a sign of their parents' continuing love for them, day in and day out.

Making Adjustments for Schedules

Of course, even though we kept our blessing simple, our busy schedules seemed to conspire to complicate matters for us. But a little flexibility helped us maintain the blessing over the years.

In biblical times certain people were considered to be endowed with a special authority to bless or to curse: priests, prophets, and fathers, for example. But a blessing could nevertheless be given by anyone. This is especially important to know as we consider establishing the blessing in our own homes today.

The primary role of blessing in our household has always rested on me as the husband and father. It's a role I've welcomed and cherished. But because of the nature of my work, I've traveled extensively throughout our life as a family and I've not always been present to give the blessing.

Knowing that anyone can give this blessing relieved some of my concern about my heavy travel schedule. Mary never begrudged my work or my schedule. She knew I was doing what I believed God wanted me to do, and she always put the best light on it for our children. She also assumed the responsibility of blessing the kids when I was gone, and often participated with me in blessing them when I was home.

When business trips would take me away from my family, adjustments had to be made. As often as possible, whether the trip was international or domestic, I would call home, hoping to catch the kids before they went to bed (when they were younger) or after they had come home (as they grew older). There was usually a bit of personal conversation with both Carlton and Lisa, and then before we ended I would bless them individually over the phone.

Frequently, if it looked to the kids as if I were going to forget—or more often, if they had to leave—they would say, "Dad, can I have my blessing now?" They weren't willing to miss it for any reason, and their commitment to the practice helped assure that the family blessing was a permanent fixture in our home.

Jesus Blessed the Children

When Jesus walked here on earth, He was subject to the same laws of physical nature as we are. When He didn't eat, He became hungry. When He didn't drink, He got thirsty. When He didn't sleep, He grew tired.

He may also have been subject to many of the same laws of *human* nature as we are. Perhaps that's why He had to get away from the crowds from time to time. As a human, He must also have tired of having the disciples around day and night for three years—I know *I* would have. He not only heard their arguing and bickering about who was going to sit where in heaven (Mark 10:35–41), but He knew their thoughts (Luke 9:46–48). Knowing what was in their hearts must have frequently caused Him some hurt.

Nevertheless, there was one group of people I'm certain Jesus would have welcomed any time. They were the children.

So often He encouraged adults to learn from the children's example, saying that we needed to be like them to enter the kingdom of God (Matthew 18:1–6). And on one very special occasion He let us see the depths of His concern for the little ones:

> Some people brought their small children to Jesus so he could touch them. But his followers told the people to stop bringing their children to him. When Jesus saw this, he was displeased. He said to them, "Let the little children come to me. Don't stop them. The kingdom of God belongs to people who are like these little children. I tell you the truth, you must accept the kingdom of God as a little child accepts things, or you will never enter it." *Then Jesus took the children in his arms. He put his hands on them and blessed them* (Mark 10:13–16, emphasis added).

Taking these children in His arms, placing His hands on them and blessing them was not at all an unfamiliar behavior to Jesus or to those around Him. He was simply doing what a good Jewish father or rabbi would have done. His action was a lesson to His listeners then and to us today about the significance of our children and the need to actively communicate God the Father to them.

An Example for Us

At times I've thought, *Oh, to have been one of those children that Jesus held in His arms and blessed.* But in all likelihood those little children were not aware of the significance of that experience. Though Jesus was the Son of God and His blessing was certainly precious, the greatest value of His one-time blessing of the children may well have been that it taught the adults who watched how they should treat their children. For those who followed His example, the most important blessings their children would receive were those they got repeatedly from their families thereafter.

Blessing our children is as vital in today's world as it was in Jesus' time. With so many temptations in our society pulling at them from so many directions, our children need a wall of protection around them. And the earlier in the lives of our children we begin strengthening that wall, the safer they'll be when the temptations come.

The wall they need is provided by our love for them. It can be reinforced, brick by brick, every time we bless them. So next we'll take a look at just how the family blessing serves to reinforce our children's sense of acceptance, security, and self-esteem.

May the Lord answer you when you are in distress;
may the name of the God of Jacob protect you.
May he send you help and grant you support.
May he give you the desire of your heart and make all
your plans succeed.
May the Lord grant all your requests.
adapted from Psalm 20:1, 2, 4, 5b, NIV

4

◇

But Does It Work?

We've seen that the family blessing is an ancient biblical practice that countless parents through the ages have maintained as valuable and even indispensable. Nevertheless, at this point I can just hear the immediate question of the typical modern business person with a concern for efficiency and effectiveness: "But does it *work?*"

No doubt we first have to clarify what we mean when we say that it "works." If we're talking about some mechanical connection between the family blessing and certain immediate, specific behaviors of our children, the relationship might be difficult to prove. And even if we *could* prove such a connection, that kind of relationship would amount to little more than manipulation.

On the other hand, a useful measure of the positive impact the family blessing has on children can be found in their own attitudes toward it in homes where it has been practiced. In our home, for example, an occasional situation has provided a telling anecdote that illustrated just how much Carlton and Lisa valued the blessing.

The Security of the Blessing

During one particular season in my life, when my work took me on many international trips lasting anywhere from two to five weeks, I simply couldn't call home to bless the children more often than once a week. On the eve of one of the longer trips, I was tucking eleven-year-old Lisa into bed when she asked, "Dad, how long will you be gone on this trip?"

"Oh," I said, "about four or five weeks."

"No," she persisted. "How many nights will you be gone—exactly?" I went to count on my calendar the exact number of nights, then returned to her room.

"Thirty-two nights," I said. "Why?"

"Well," Lisa mused, "then you have to give me thirty-two blessings. Now."

I chuckled as I considered her request, but I thought, *Why not?* So I agreed: "Let's do it!"

Anticipating that this would take a while, I lay down beside her as I placed my hand on her head. Then I began: "The Lord bless you and keep you, Lisa. . . ." I went on to say the full blessing from Numbers 6:24–26 that I had spoken over her for years.

When I was done, Lisa said, "That's one, Dad. You've got thirty-one more to go!"

Many minutes later, when I finished the last one (with Lisa counting all the way), she chirped, "Okay, Dad. Now you can go on your trip." The job was done. Lisa felt secure. She knew everything would be all right, even when Dad was a long way from home. His blessing for every night represented to her the security of his commitment to her welfare.

Children Blessing Each Other

Over the years, Mary and I were out so late on some evenings that Carlton and Lisa had to go to bed without us. So when we came home, I would quietly enter their rooms, place my hand on each one of their heads, kiss them on the cheek, and bless them.

On these occasions, the importance of the blessing to them was usually affirmed the next morning at breakfast when they would tell us how they had blessed each other before they went to bed. In what was to them a perfectly natural procedure, they had placed their hands on each other's head, just as we had done to them so many times before.

At other times, when Lisa's blessing was over, she would

say, "Wait, Dad." Then she would place her little hand on my head and return the blessing. Those times were always spontaneous and always welcome, but never expected. It was simply Lisa's way of saying, "This is so good, Dad, that I don't want you to miss out on it." And I'm forever grateful.

"Don't Forget the Power and Protection!"

As you consider how these children's positive attitudes toward the family blessing indicate its significance in their lives, you might reasonably wonder whether the particular words spoken in a blessing really mean anything to the children themselves, especially if they're young. You might even conclude that all the kids are actually responding to is the simple fact that they're receiving a few regular minutes of parental attention which they might not otherwise get.

I would agree that one critical factor in the blessing's ability to convey God's love to kids is this element of parental attention, which they desperately need. But at the same time, many children—even younger ones—apparently listen carefully to what's being said.

My friend Paul Thigpen has been blessing his children every night for several years now. He began one night with a simple "God bless you with grace and peace in Jesus' name. Amen." But over the following few months, as he thought about all the particular kinds of blessing he wanted his children to experience, the list grew. Now each night he lays his hands on his children and says:

> *God bless you with grace and peace,*
> *power and protection*
> *health and healing,*
> *holiness and godliness,*
> *abundance and prosperity,*
> *and all the fruit and gifts of the Holy Spirit,*
> *in Jesus' name, Amen.*

That's a formidable list of blessings to remember, even for an adult, and it's only because Paul repeats them every night that he's able to call them to mind without a "cheat sheet."

Nevertheless, one evening last year Paul was exhausted from a particularly demanding day, and as he blessed his children, he accidentally forgot the second pair of blessings, saying, ". . . grace and peace, health and healing . . ." Immediately his six-year-old daughter, Lydia, interrupted.

"*Dad,*" she insisted, "don't forget the *power and protection.* That's important!"

Even a six-year-old was paying close attention, caught the oversight, remembered the missing phrase, and knew that every word was important. Needless to say, Paul has never forgotten "power and protection" since!

No *Instantaneous Growth*

In our automated, computerized, high-tech world we're becoming more and more conditioned to expect the instantaneous. First it was the instant camera, giving us a developed picture in about five minutes. But then, who wanted to wait five minutes? So soon it was sixty seconds. Still too slow. Now it only takes about ten seconds, and researchers are trying to shorten even that.

Next came instant mashed potatoes, instant coffee, instant this and instant that. None of these "improvements" seem to me to be as good as the real thing. They may be close. They may even look and smell similar. But you can tell the difference. For that reason, I'm a little skeptical of techniques that promise instant changes in our children. No doubt the results of blessing our children, or anyone else, are *sometimes* visible immediately. In the next chapter, in fact, you'll hear the story of one family that experienced immediate results from the blessing during a time of deep crisis. But usually we only see the results of the family blessing much later. And sometimes only God sees these results.

The Chinese Bamboo Tree

Zig Ziglar tells the story of the Chinese bamboo tree. When the seed of this tree is planted, it acts in a way other seeds don't: Instead of sending up a shoot, it goes dormant. No amount of nurture and attention can rouse it from its sleep.

Zig says that the Chinese bamboo lies in its dormant state for five years with no apparent signs of growth. Then in one year it suddenly grows over sixty feet into a mature tree.

Even though the tree reveals no visible signs of growth for several years, it still requires all the care that would be given to any other seed. Without such care during its incubation, it would never become a tree. Since the farmers know this, they continue doing what they know is right to care for the seed— despite the lack of any visible results to encourage them.

Kids can be like Chinese bamboo trees. As parents we may do everything we know is right for them, but then we may despair if we don't see any immediate growth or change of heart. Sometimes we even become so anxious over their development that we "dig them up" with our frustration and undo the good we've done.

This situation may be especially frustrating when a child once made a commitment to the Lord at an early age. Often when the transition time of the teen-age years arrives, that sweet, obedient child may begin to question and rebel against both us and our faith. They may even appear to be going headlong in the wrong direction, doing things they know are wrong.

How should a parent respond when that happens? Do you force them to accept your faith "or else . . ."? Or do you keep on "hoeing" around them, tending to the things you know will produce a mature tree someday?

Though it's easy to give up at such a time, we must keep in mind that we really want our kids to have their *own* faith in God, not their *parents'* faith. Sometimes the transfer of this faith is swift and smooth; sometimes it's slow and painful. But if we keep on doing what we know is right, sooner or later the tree will grow, and when it does it will be strong and well-rooted.

Your commitment to giving the blessing to your children during these difficult months or years shows them a side of your faith they might never see otherwise: the side of patience in adversity. Your steady, unwavering demonstration of your confidence in what they'll become will help them rise to those positive expectations.

Eternal Investments

In the business world we have something we call "R.O.I."—which stands for "return on investment." The bottom line in business is that if the return isn't greater than the investment, we don't do it. Everything must be quantified. We're always asking, "If I put this in here, how much will I get back over here?"

When I do business, I try to work within these parameters. But when, like Jesus, I go "about my Father's business," and I'm dealing with spiritual values, the "return on investment" must be measured in terms of *eternal* investment. I may not see all the rewards of my efforts until the whole story of life is told. But I must be faithful to continue doing what I know is right.

The Benefits of the Blessing

Now having pointed out all of that, I still want to affirm that God *does* desire to lavish Himself on us and to reward our obedience to Him openly and abundantly—and sometimes quickly. He has many ways He can and does do just that, as His promises indicate: He will meet all our needs (Philippians 4:19); He will give us the desires of our hearts (Psalm 37:4); He will send angels to guard us (Psalm 91:11); He will withhold no good thing (Psalm 84:11).

One of the great benefits of the family blessing that we have seen in our own children over a period of years is an openness and honesty in them, both toward us and toward God. This has been illustrated repeatedly by the candor they've shown in voluntarily confessing to us things they've done that they knew were wrong.

I still remember how on one particular night when Carlton was about eleven years old, he called us to his room. We had tucked him in for the night, prayed with him, and given him his "hands-on" blessing about an hour earlier. But alone in the dark of his room he had been thinking about something he had done that day. He knew in his heart that what he had done was wrong, and God would not, as the blessing said, "give him peace" until he confessed his sin and made things right.

When we entered his room, it didn't take long for the confession to come and the tears of repentance to flow freely. We listened as he prayed and asked God to forgive him and help him not to disobey again. We talked with him about what he had done and let him know that God had heard his prayer and forgiven him. As his parents, we verbally forgave him, too. Then we prayed again with him and left.

As we were walking to the door of his bedroom, he said, "I feel like a big bag of junk just left me!" Mary and I rejoiced with him in his release from this guilt, and knew that God was at work in him. Since that time, we have marveled again and again at how both Carlton and Lisa have remained open with us about what's going on in their lives.

The Impact on Our Own Behavior

My wife and I have seen the benefits of blessing our kids, not just in how they behave, but in how we respond to their behavior as well. Earlier we noted that as Christian parents, our greatest responsibility to *God* is to raise our children to know and love Him with all their hearts. At the same time, our greatest responsibility to *our children* is to exhibit the heart of God to them. What they see in us has great bearing on what they understand God to be like.

When we have something we dearly treasure, we take special care of it, making certain that it's not damaged or destroyed. We accord it a place of honor and would never consider taking out our frustration or anger on such a treasure. Instead, we protect it in every way possible.

The same is true of our children. After years of reinforcing their sense of security, acceptance, and self-esteem through the family blessing, the last thing we want to do is destroy what we've worked so diligently to cultivate. So the act of blessing our children becomes a daily reminder that we have built a relationship with them and an attitude within them that must be protected—even when we have reason to be angry with them.

Back in 1981 I bought a new car that was easily the nicest car I had ever owned—and certainly the most expensive. I loved it! I was proud of it and took special care of it, washing it frequently and maintaining it faithfully.

One day in the early spring, however, I noticed a footprint on the hood as I entered the garage to leave for work. Upon closer inspection, I also saw a *dent* in the hood where the footprint was.

There was little question that it was Carlton's footprint. My heart sank and my anger rose. I thought of all sorts of names other than Carlton to use on him at that moment. But I'm grateful now that he had already left for school so I couldn't use them!

As I stood by the front of the car, I wondered why he would have stood on the hood. Then I saw my golf clubs on the shelf above the front of the car, remembered the warm spring weather, and understood.

As I drove to work, I noticed that the dent in the hood was right in my line of vision so that every time I sat behind the steering wheel of that car, I would see it. Because it was in such a prominent place, my immediate thought was to get it fixed. After all, wasn't that what I had insurance for?

Nevertheless, I heard the Lord saying, "Just leave it. It's not that bad, and besides, the car's not yours anyway. It's *mine*. Everything you have is *mine*. And so is your family."

I thought of the close relationship I'd built with my son, and how much I treasured him. Then I thought of how close I'd come to allowing something else I treasured—something of infinitely less value—to hurt that relationship. I had blessed my son for years; was I going to "curse" him with hurtful words now?

No. Instead, I heard God saying, "Why not use that dent as a positive reminder that your son needs your prayer?" After all, the Lord had given me this boy so I could care for him, pray for him, and show him the heart of his heavenly Father.

Last year that old car finally expired. It had clocked 128,000 miles by the time it died, and nearly as many prayers of gratitude for God's goodness in giving me that son.

By the way—when I did question Carlton about the dent, he had no idea of what he'd done. He'd simply acted impulsively on the desire to swing the golf clubs. So he apologized, asked me to forgive him, and agreed to use the stepladder next time. Needless to say, our relationship was stronger than ever before.

A Model Young Woman

All the examples of the blessing's long-term benefits need not come from our family. I still remember how in 1974, when we were still living in Puerto Rico, we received a letter from Laurie Christenson (now Laurie Kuck), Larry and Nordis's seventeen-year-old daughter. In it she asked whether she and two of her friends from church could come to Puerto Rico to spend the summer with us. We were thrilled to have them come, so a few months later they arrived.

Mary and I had been married over six years and had been in charge of the mission there for over five. We had seen a number of young people come and go during our time there. Some came just for a visit; some used their summer to gain exposure to missionary life; others stayed a year or longer, filling vital roles in that work.

They were your normal mix of kids. Some were serious about their experience. Others just wanted to get it over with. Some were diligent in what they did, while others just wanted to have fun. Some were adventurers, always looking for the next challenge. Others seldom left the mission. Some sought to learn the customs and language of the Puerto Rican people, while others stayed to themselves.

Whatever their individual style, we loved them all. Laurie, however, stood out as someone special. She exemplified a long list of admirable character qualities, impressing us with a maturity beyond what was typical of her age. But there was something else about her as well, something that came from deep inside her and touched all those she met.

Laurie, you see, had grown up with the uncompromising love of her parents—a love shown to her, among many other ways, by the family blessing, spoken to her every night for years. As Mary and I observed her throughout that summer, we became more convinced than ever of the rightness of blessing our children as Laurie had been blessed. In her, we were seeing the long-term fruit of the family blessing.

It Works!

Does the blessing of your children "work"? Is it worth the time and commitment? The answer is clear: Yes! Absolutely! Or, as we Scandinavians here in Minnesota like to say, "Ya, sure, you betcha!"

Our experience and that of many other families shows that the blessing "works." Of course, just *how* it works is a bit more difficult to explain. We can point to the sense of security and concern that is obviously produced by speaking words of encouragement to a child, day after day, and recognize that such encouragement is bound to impact the child's life for good. But the family blessing seems to convey much more.

As the ancient Hebrews recognized, words of blessing spoken in the name of God are somehow able to transmit the power and favor of God. That is simply a mystery which we must accept, and for which we must be grateful.

However the blessing works, those who have faithfully spoken it year after year would probably all agree on one point: We practice the family blessing *because it is right*. And because it is right, God rewards those who bless.

Ultimately, the question is not "Does it work?" but rather, "Should I open myself up to the mystery of what God wants to do in and through me by committing myself to the blessing?" We do it in good faith, leaving the results to Him. And sometimes, as we'll see in the next chapter, those results are even more than we could hope for.

May the God who gives endurance and encouragement give you a spirit of unity among yourselves as you follow Christ Jesus, so that with one heart and mouth you may glorify the God and Father of our Lord Jesus Christ.

May the God of all hope fill you with all joy and peace as you trust in him, so that you may overflow with hope by the power of the Holy Spirit.

The God of peace be with you all.

Romans 15:5, 6, 13, 33, NIV

5

◇

*The Marci
Straley Story*

During our ten years as literature missionaries in Puerto Rico, Mary and I enjoyed meeting the hundreds of customers who shopped at our store. Some were just casual acquaintances—people who came in once in a while to buy a book or Bible. Others took time to let us get to know them as friends through times of prayer, sharing, and laughter together. We loved to see them come in—even if they didn't buy anything!

A few became a precious part of our lives. These were the ones who worshiped with us at the midweek Bible study I led on the upstairs open patio of the bookstore. They shared meals with us, helped us out in practical ways, and never asked anything in return. Their love was pure and deep.

The Straley Family

Dan and Joy Straley were two of these special friends. They lived at Fort Buchanan Army Base in San Juan with their three girls—Lisa, Marci, and Andrea—and an enormous basset hound named Buffy.

Dan was quick-witted, spontaneous, fun-loving, and just nuts enough to keep you wondering what was coming next. He was game for anything, and if nothing was going on, he would come up with something. Everyone loved him.

Dan was also a loving husband, caring father, and industrious provider for his family. He loved the Lord with all his heart and desired to share Him with others, including his kids.

Joy was the stabilizer in the Straley home. Her steady, solid, diligent nature brought order to their world, and she had a warmth that came from a heart the size of Texas.

When Dan and Joy began attending our Wednesday night Bible studies, they often brought their girls with them. The two oldest, Lisa and Marci, were about the same ages as our two children (five and three), and the four of them had little trouble getting along. Andrea, who was born in Puerto Rico, was just an infant.

One Wednesday night during the middle of the meeting, my son padded out onto the crowded patio in his footed pajamas, came right up to where I was standing, and stretched out his arms for a good-night hug and blessing. So I stopped a moment, knelt down by him, gave him his hug, placed my hands on his head, and quietly spoke to him his nightly blessing. When I finished, I kissed him on the cheek, and he ran off to bed.

After the meeting, Dan asked me about what had happened. He saw that this practice was more important to both Carlton and me than anything else at that moment, and he wanted to know all about it. So I told him about our experience with Larry Christenson and his daughter Laurie, and explained how the practice had become a part of our family. Dan seemed receptive to the idea, and as I recall, we never discussed it again.

A Blessing for Special Occasions

Throughout the past fifteen years, we've maintained a close friendship with the Straleys that has provided us with countless moments of laughter and joy, as well as times of tears and heartache. During that time, Dan established his own practice of blessing his children.

The Straleys' family blessing is different than ours, however, in one particular way. While I felt I should bless my kids every night, Dan reserved his blessing for important occasions. He feels that the blessing is a special gift from God, wrapped by Dad, and given to the child as God directs. So he pronounces the blessing when a particular event or situation calls for a special deepening and strengthening of emotional ties with his daughters.

A couple of years ago, for example, Lisa was leaving home to attend college. Mom and Dad were emotional wrecks; after all, she was their firstborn and the first to leave home. Lisa, on the other hand, was alive with excitement at the thought of meeting new friends, getting out on her own, and making plans for her adult life. While Mom and Dad were choking back the tears, Lisa was nearly squealing with delight over her future.

Once they arrived with Lisa's things on campus, she took care of registration, found her new dorm room, and got settled in with the rest of the family's help. Then they said their good-byes.

Just before the Straleys got into their car to drive home, Dan hugged Lisa. As he did, he placed his hands on her head and declared to her, "Lisa, the Lord bless you and keep you. The Lord make His face shine upon you, and be gracious unto you. The Lord lift up His countenance upon you, and give you peace. In the name of the Father, and of the Son, and of the Holy Spirit. Amen."

As Daddy spoke the family blessing, all Lisa's resolve to be "grown up" and not to cry went bouncing down her cheeks. It was okay now. Dad had not only given *his* blessing on this big step in her life, but now he had invoked *God's* blessing on her, too.

These times of family blessing in the Straley household may have been given sparingly. But when they were given, the results were always the same: Those involved experienced an acute sense of God's presence accompanied by rivers of tears, then followed by the quiet, calming awareness of God's peace.

Marci's Special Blessing

The Straleys' middle daughter, Marci, is the kind of person who brightens the life of all she meets, lightening their load with her buoyant spirit and genuine love. The harshest criticism Marci ever received from her teachers at school was that "she's altogether too happy—she laughs too much!"

To Marci, everything is funny. Dan claims: "When the doctor spanked Marci at birth, she didn't cry. She laughed!" Her eyes twinkle with that I-know-something-you-don't-know-and-you-won't-find-out-until-it-happens look.

About a year and a half after Lisa went off to school, Marci turned eighteen. She was finishing her senior year of high school and already well into her plans for attending Southern Nazarene University (SNU) in Bethany, Oklahoma, where Lisa was a sophomore. Marci couldn't wait to join her sister on campus; she had dreamed of that day for years, and now it was almost in reach.

One day, however, Marci began to experience some pain in breathing and in her side. It lasted for a few days, but it didn't seem serious, so she wasn't too concerned. When she went to a doctor to be examined, he said, "It looks like you have a good case of 'mono,' young lady," and told her to rest. She did, but as the days went by and the pain continued, both she and her parents became convinced that something was very wrong.

They went to a second doctor, who put Marci through a battery of tests. It was obvious by the type of tests he was giving that he was concerned about what he was finding. But until all the results were in, he wouldn't speculate on what it was. After she had a CAT scan at the hospital, she and Dan went to find out the results.

They were fearful about what they would be told, but prayed that God would have His way. As they entered the doctor's office for once in her life Marci wasn't laughing. They sat in silence as the doctor gave his report.

"The news isn't good," he said, directing his comments to Dan. "We've found seven spots on Marci's liver and what appears to be a tumor on her pancreas. We've also found other spots on her spleen and lungs. We'll need to do a biopsy."

Three days later when the results of the biopsy came in, Dan and Joy asked the doctors if they could give Marci the report after they took her home. He agreed. Later that evening while sitting together on their bed, Dan and Joy carefully told her the news that the tumor she had was malignant.

Hoping for the best while fearing the worst, Marci asked, "Is that bad? What does that mean?"

"It means you have cancer, Marci," Dan said soberly. Instantly, both Marci and her parents burst into convulsive sobs as the words were finally spoken. The silent, carefully camouflaged fears were now exposed, and they were terrified. When Dan regained his composure, he continued, "They have to operate very soon."

The family had little rest that night or the next several nights as uncontrollable waves of emotion tossed in their minds. The days were filled with work, making arrangements, phoning friends, and prayer. The night hours were filled alternately with silence and questions: "What is Your will, God? Would You bring her this far just to take her now? Why Marci?"

Dan called Mary and me the first night after the doctor's report to tell us of the situation. We listened. We wept. We ached. And we prayed. It was the first of many calls between us about Marci's condition.

Dan kept us abreast both of the medical situation and of the emotional tug-of-war raging in his heart and mind. He told of dreams he saw being crushed, both Marci's dreams and those of her family for her.

As the date for Marci's surgery came, her parents, pastor, and closest friends joined her in the hospital to pray and support one another. Dan said the only way he could hold together during that time was to say the name of Jesus over and over in his mind. The thought of his eighteen-year-old daughter having cancer was almost more than he could bear.

Everyone gathered around Marci's bed as the time of reckoning drew close. The anxiety and grief were overwhelming. As they stood around her bed, ten people joined hands to pray, but they could only cry.

At last the orderly came for Marci, but just before she was to be rolled out of her hospital room for surgery, Dan leaned over her. Wrapping his arms gently around her, he gave her a hug. Then reaching up, he held her head firmly in both his hands and whispered to Marci that very special blessing. Slowly, clearly, and with a level of faith and conviction he had never felt before, he spoke God's favor and power into her once more.

"Marci, the Lord bless you, dear child, and keep you. . . ." Even as he spoke the words, he knew God was honoring his request. "The Lord make His face shine upon you, Marci, and be gracious unto you. . . ." He could feel Marci's head relax in his hands as he continued. "The Lord lift up His countenance upon you and give you peace!" And then, almost as a verbal exclamation point, he said, "In the name of the Father, and of His Son, Jesus, and of the Holy Spirit, Amen!"

When he finished, Marci looked him in the eye and smiled. "It's okay now, Daddy," she assured him. "Everything's going to be all right."

The fear that had gripped the rest of those in the room had now turned to faith. In the waiting room, where they hoped to be hearing good news shortly, they continued praying and encouraging each other.

The operation was scheduled to last three hours. But within forty-five minutes, the doctor came out of surgery to where the family was gathered. He fumbled for words and finally said, "I'm sorry. When we opened Marci up, we found that the cancer had spread to her intestines and her endocrine system, and that the pancreas is nearly three times its normal size because of the tumor. We have done all we can do."

When Joy heard the chilling words, she collapsed. Dan caught her and set her down, then slumped to the floor himself. The others gathered around them. No one said a word. There were no words that could possibly express their disappointment. They just held on to Dan and Joy—and wept.

When Marci was finally rolled out of surgery, she was hooked up to more tubes, monitors, and various other types of apparatus than any of the family and friends could imagine. *What next?* they thought. *Would she even live? How much would she be able to take?*

But then, like a great wave of comfort, the Lord flooded over Dan and Joy. They were exhausted from many sleepless nights and continual anxiety. But as this wave washed over them, it brought strength—spiritual, emotional, and physical. With it God gave them peace and rest. And then, in an almost audible voice, Dan heard God say to him, "Just as you have blessed your daughter, I am blessing you. Let go of your grief. Cross this sea of anguish on dry ground." And they did.

I have never seen such peace, faith, strength, and even joy in the face of such a crushing blow. Just as the Lord had granted Marci supernatural grace and peace through the family blessing her father had spoken, her family and friends were now standing strong in the knowledge of God's word of blessing to them.

Marci's Recovery

Pancreatic cancer is the most deadly form known and extremely rare in a young person. As high as 92 percent of such cases prove fatal. Marci and her family were told there was no possible cure for her, and the best they could hope for was a 50-percent chance of stabilizing the growth.

Since the day of her surgery, Marci has been receiving chemotherapy. At the time of this writing, she has been treated for about seven months. In that period her recovery has been amazing. All the spots of cancer on her lungs and intestines are gone. The two on her liver are the size of BBs, much reduced from when the treatment started.

And her pancreas has shrunk to very near its normal size.

Marci's doctors could not be more thrilled with her progress. Her family and friends are confident that the God who has begun a good work in her will complete it.

A Channel of God's Goodness

Last night I called Dan to go over some of the details of Marci's story. I told him I had left the name of their city out of this chapter to protect their privacy. He said, "Rolf, if we can encourage one other person to trust God in tough times, if we can help one person through some deep waters by sharing with them what God has done for us, then put our address, home phone number—even my work phone number—in the book." So I'm doing precisely that—the information appears at the bottom of this page. My request is that you uphold all the Straley family—Dan, Joy, Lisa, Marci, and Andrea—in prayer as God lays them on your heart. Marci is feeling great these days. She's working and even bought a used car recently.

As you might guess, the chemotherapy has caused Marci to lose her hair. But even that has been a source of laughter for her. After the first treatment, she came home and announced, "Hey, Mom—you know how you've always wanted to cut my hair? Well, now's your chance. It's all going to fall out soon anyway!" Even now, just for laughs, when she sees a stranger in a restaurant staring at the turban on her head, she reaches up and yanks it off, revealing her bald, fuzzy head, before the stranger can look away. The joy of this young woman who is confident of God's love and her family's love is as irrepressible as ever.

"In the midst of all the ups and downs of the last few months," Dan reaffirmed, "we have been soaked—marinated, if you will—in God's goodness, to make us more tender toward Him." Marci's story illustrates powerfully how the family blessing played a significant part in channeling that divine goodness into the life of the Straley family when they needed it most.

Dan and Joy Straley
1427 Bradford Place
Mesquite, Texas 75149
214-289-3974 (home)
214-956-9712 (Dan's work number)

Blessed is the man who fears the Lord,
who finds great delight in his commands.
His children will be mighty in the land;
the generation of the upright will be blessed.
Wealth and riches are in his house,
and his righteousness endures forever.
Even in darkness, light dawns for the upright,
for the gracious and compassionate and righteous man.
Surely he will never be shaken;
a righteous man will be remembered forever.
                    Psalm 112:1b, 2, 3, 4, 6, NIV

6

◇

Feedback from the Kids

The parents I know who practice the family blessing have no doubt in their own minds that it makes a significant difference in the lives of their children. But perhaps the most convincing testimonies of what the blessing can mean come from the children themselves. For that reason, this chapter simply presents what several older children have to say in their own words about what it was like to grow up being blessed by their parents.

The first two letters are from my own children, Carlton and Lisa. The next three are from Tim, Robert, and Kristi Lenning. Their father, Larry Lenning, is co-pastor at Immanuel Lutheran Church in Independence, Iowa, and the author of *Blessing in Mosque and Mission,* which includes an excellent survey of the blessings in the Bible and the history of the church. The next two are from Tonia Douglas and Pam Cooley, friends of our family. And the last two are from Laurie Kuck, Larry Christenson's daughter, and Lisa Straley, Marci's sister.

Dear Dad,

Let me start out by saying that I love you very much. I have nothing but respect for you. As a child growing up, there is no one a son looks up to more than his dad. The love and attention you showed me meant so much. I always felt I could tell you anything.

This was shown especially in your blessings, which I had every night for as long as I can remember There is so much more involved in those blessings than just the words themselves. I want you to know that when you came into my room to bless me, I felt very special. It only established my confidence and made me feel worthwhile. It made me feel that you were behind me 100 percent and that you trusted me and gave me your blessing on everything I did. When you told me to do something—for instance, to be home by a certain time—I wanted to obey because I didn't want to break your trust.

Well, obviously, I'm not the second person to lead a perfect life. I've made more than a handful of bad decisions and choices. Yet despite that, you are always forgiving and there to listen to my problems.

I consider you both a friend and a role model. I have always had fun with you. Whether it was when you were taking me out to play baseball and golf or going to my baseball games religiously, I felt great to have you there to watch me play all those years. We would go home, talk about the game, and you would listen to me brag about what a great catch or hit I made. I also enjoyed watching football with you every Sunday as we groaned, booed, and cheered the Vikings on. After the game was always the best, because I would be so keyed up to play football that we would go outside, where I would run you ragged for an hour.

It's things like that that make me realize you're not just blowing smoke when you say, "The Lord bless you and keep you, the Lord make His face shine upon you and be gracious to you, the Lord lift up His countenance upon you and give you peace, in the name of the Father, and of the Son, and of the Holy Spirit." It shows me that you really mean what you say—that I am special to you.

Actions speak so much louder than words. I can tell by the way you bless and treat me that you love me. That constant reminder every night is very special to me. Thank you for your unconditional love. It means more to me than you'll ever know.

Carlton
age twenty-one

Dear Dad and Mom,

Thank you so much for committing to the task of blessing me every night—every night since I can remember. Those words that began, "The Lord bless you and keep you . . ." were short, but wow! so powerful and comforting all at the same time. Many times as I stood there, it was as if the Lord Himself were speaking straight to me. They were words of encouragement that made me feel so special and so loved.

I loved to have friends come and stay overnight because you would always bless them right along with me. After you left the room they would often remark on how awesome it was to receive a blessing.

Dad, I will never forget the night you blessed me thirty-two times before you left on a trip for that many days. I know that was going a little overboard on my part and probably not necessary, but at that time it put me at ease that you took the time to repeat the blessing thirty-two times in a row while I carefully kept track. I'll also never forget all the times you have called me from far-off countries while you've been on business trips just to talk to me and give me a blessing.

One other thing that really stands out is the time you made a tape recording before you left on an overseas trip so we could play it every night you were gone. It was so sweet and contained words of affirmation and encouragement, a prayer for God's protection, and then a blessing for Mom, Carlton and me. All of these special times will stick with me forever.

Mom, your involvement in giving me a blessing has meant a lot as well. You always faithfully filled in for Dad if he was gone late, or on a trip; even when he was home, you would often still bless me anyway. I guess I was really lucky to receive two blessings a night sometimes.

Now that I'm away at college, I've come to appreciate the blessing more than ever. When I first left, I was worried because I thought I wasn't going to be blessed anymore. But I now know that being away doesn't mean you've quit blessing me. I've come to understand that your hands don't have to be on my head, and we don't even need to be standing in the same room for me to receive the blessing that I know you still give me every night. It's extra special now when you bless me over the phone at the end of one of our numerous daily phone calls and every time I see you in person.

Thank you again for loving and caring for me enough to make the unique commitment of blessing me every night. I can assure you that your efforts have not been in vain. I believe the blessing is one of the biggest reasons for the close relationship we share. It's a time of bonding and security that I'll always cherish. I love you both so much.

Lisa
age eighteen

Dear Mr. Garborg,

I was two or three years old and not sleeping very well when my parents began blessing me every night before going to bed. They would say: "The grace of Jesus Christ, and the love of God the Father, and the fellowship of the Holy Spirit, be with you always, Timmy." One simple yet powerful sentence—and it helped me sleep better. I know I didn't pay much attention to the words at that age, but the feeling of love—God's love as well as my parents' love—was very reassuring.

As time passed, I began to rely on being blessed every night. I can even remember on more than one occasion calling my mom and dad into the bedroom and asking for the blessing they had forgotten to give me earlier. Without my blessing, something was missing. The day just wasn't complete.

As I grew older and my faith began to grow, the words of blessing took on a new meaning. They reinforced what I was learning in Sunday school and confirmation class, and testified to my parents' faith. These factors helped me to grow in my faith and my relationship with God through those rocky times of being a teenager.

I am not too sure when I stopped receiving my nightly blessing, but I've never forgotten it. Now that I'm married, and children will be on the way in four or five years, I know that my wife and I will pass on that blessing of "the grace of Jesus Christ, the love of God the Father, and the fellowship of the Holy Spirit."

Tim Lenning
age twenty-three

Dear Mr. Garborg,

As a younger child, probably right up to the age of thirteen or fourteen, I was blessed by both of my parents right before I would go to sleep each night. If they would forget, I would usually remind them to make sure that I got their blessing.

As I recall what I thought about while they blessed me, I realize that the blessing meant several different things. The first thing was that it was sort of like my parents telling me that I was all right. It was a sign of their love, and it improved my self-esteem. And not only was I accepted by them, but by God as well. It was as if God were talking through my parents, telling me that He will always be with me and He will always love me, no matter what I go through.

Both God and my parents were telling me that I was loved and that they will always be there for me.

A second thing that came from the blessing was a kind of security from my parents. By being blessed right before bedtime, I was able to sleep better, knowing that I was safe because both God and my parents were watching over me. This helped me through many nightmares and times when I thought monsters were under my bed!

I realize even more now how powerful the blessing of God is, and I plan to do the same thing for my children.

Robert Lenning
age twenty

Dear Mr. Garborg,

When I was little, my parents blessed me every night before I went to sleep. It always made me feel secure and loved. Sometimes my parents got too busy at night and so they would forget. But I would go to both of them, put my head in their laps, and tell them they forgot. I usually couldn't go to sleep if I wasn't blessed.

The blessing was sort of like a hug to my head. If I had friends over, my parents would bless them, too. I thought if they didn't get blessed, they would have a nightmare or not be able to sleep. I also made them bless my dog. He was as special as my friends. Sometimes after I had been blessed and tucked in, I would bless my dog as if he were my own child.

I don't get blessed any more. One night, though, I was really upset. My life was in the dumps. I had been crying for about an hour, and Mom told me it was time to go to bed. So she came then and blessed me. It didn't make me feel childish. Instead, it reminded me that I was loved and that I had many things going for me.

I know that when I have kids, I'll do the same for them as my parents did for me.

Kristi Lenning
age fifteen

Dear Mr. Garborg,

The words of our family blessing have always had special meaning to me. We use Aaron's blessing from Numbers 6.

First of all, through all these years of receiving the blessing from both my parents every night before I go to bed—and every morning before I go to school—I have always felt a certain sense of security and protection. No matter where I go or wherever I am—even when I'm out of town—I know the Lord will, as my parents' words say, "bless me and keep me."

Because of my parents' love and their blessing me twice a day, three hundred and sixty-five days a year, year after year, I have always felt especially loved by the Lord. I've always felt that God truly was "making His face to shine" upon me and being "gracious" to me.

Because the Lord has "lifted up His countenance" on me and shown me who He really is, I've always had a special interest in the things of God: reading the Bible, praying, and just spending time with Him.

And I've always had the deep inner sense that God had "given me peace," a peace that remains with me constantly.

Because my earthly father blesses me daily, I'm reminded of how my heavenly Father blesses me daily. I have a good rapport with my father, and it helps me have a healthy relationship with my heavenly Father as well.

Tonia Douglas
age eighteen

Dear Mom,

I'm writing this letter to express my gratefulness to you for your consistency to pray for me. Prayer is so effective, and I believe that God has honored your prayers and protected me.

Mom, the blessing you prayed over Kim and me every day will always be a fond and vivid memory of my childhood:

> Now unto Him who is able to keep you from falling, and to present you faultless before the presence of His glory with exceeding joy, to the only wise God our Savior, be glory and majesty, dominion and power, both now and ever. Amen. (Jude 1:24–25, KJV).

I remember that Dad would say that blessing over us each night. Then after he died, you started saying it over us. It was hard for us and I'm sure painful for you, because it brought back memories. But I'm so glad you continued that prayer.

Kim and I could repeat it but we didn't understand the words. Even so, I knew it was important. I liked when you prayed aloud over us. It made me feel safe. I knew I was being watched over by my heavenly Father.

This blessing states God's ability to protect and keep us, and it's a powerful prayer. You can probably remember the times that you forgot, and how we would yell from our beds that we wanted you to say the blessing over us—even in our high school years. I guess I felt I could sleep better knowing I was in Jesus' care.

Mom, thank you for your commitment to Jesus in praying for us with faithfulness and consistency. This has deeply affected my life and I believe it has protected me from many things.

Because this blessing has been a part of my life, I can't imagine leaving it out in my future family. Mom, thank you for instilling in me the importance of prayer and of committing a child to God's care. I love you.

Pam Cooley
age twenty

Dear Mr. Garborg,

My memories of the family blessing are a mixture of all that it meant to go to bed as a child. Dad's blessing was always preceded by Mom's coming in to scratch our backs and sing a song to us. Then Dad would say the benediction over us. If I'd gone to sleep, I remember often rousing just enough to hear the words before going to sleep.

I think that the daily repetition of that activity provided a great security for me. I knew I was in a protected place. As an adult now I appreciate how my parents relied on the heavenly Father to provide that protection for our family.

I've recently married and I look forward to providing that same security for our children.

Laurie Kuck
age thirty-two

Dear Mom and Dad,

When Mr. Garborg first asked me to write a letter telling what the family blessing has meant to me, I was both very excited and honored. After all, this looked to be an excellent opportunity for me to express my love and appreciation to you both for the wonderful Christian guidance that you've given me.

But now that the time has come actually to write down my feelings, I find myself struggling to pull all the right words together.

The blessing has given me security, encouragement, confidence, courage, peace—I could go on and on. But it isn't just the words alone that draw out those feelings. Much of it—no, ninety-nine percent of it—has to do with *who* is actually pronouncing the blessing. *That* is what makes it so very, very special to me.

I can't honestly say that I remember when you first pronounced the blessing on me. But I do remember the times when it has meant the most. One time in particular comes to mind.

Being the oldest child in our family, I'm usually the first one to experience life's little traumas. Perhaps the most eye-opening of my experiences happened two and a half years ago, when I moved away from home to go to college. I'll have to admit, Mom and Dad, that I was pretty excited that day (okay, *very* excited). But as the day wore on and the time for you to leave came closer and closer, reality began to sink in. It hit me that I wasn't going back home with you this time.

My sadness only intensified as the hours went by until the good-byes were being said. It was during this vulnerable time, Dad, that you took my hands in yours, bowed your head, and pronounced the most reverent and awe-inspiring blessing that I have ever heard. The tears were flowing fast.

I still remember the calm that came over me when you finished blessing me. I suddenly had a peace about the future. I felt the courage to face the days to come, knowing that God would, in some way, provide all the answers to my unasked questions. And yet, through all this "instant" maturity, I felt at the same time secure in the knowledge that you both would be there for me whenever I needed you—and that's the best security of all. All of these emotions had been inside of me, fighting for some semblance of order in my mind, but they came to life only after your sincere utterance of that powerful prayer.

I did a lot of growing up that day. And thanks to you both, the blessing proved to be the stepping stone on which I took my first tentative step out into life.

Thanks, Mom and Dad, for your loving guidance and your Christian example. If I'm only half as good at parenting as you two are, then I'll consider myself a success. I love you both very much!

Lisa Straley
age twenty-one

What the book of Proverbs says about the godly wife and mother can evidently be applied to both parents when they convey God's grace to their children through the family blessing. In these testimonial letters we see illustrated powerfully and beautifully that scriptural promise: Their children shall rise up and *bless* them (Proverbs 31:28). In that way, the blessing given becomes as well a blessing received.

May God himself, the God of peace, sanctify you through and through. May your whole spirit, soul and body be kept blameless at the coming of our Lord Jesus Christ. The one who calls you is faithful, and he will do it. The grace of our Lord Jesus Christ be with you.
1 Thessalonians 5:23, 24, 28, NIV

7

◇

Getting Started

The most difficult part of any job for me is getting started. I will procrastinate, postpone, delay, and avoid starting just as long as I can. In fact, I will even do several other jobs to avoid beginning on the first. And I sense that I'm not alone in this regard.

Sometimes the tasks I delay are as simple as replacing a burned-out light bulb. I can rationalize, justify, excuse, and defend this behavior with brilliant comments like, "We can see just fine without that light," or "Do you realize how much it costs to burn that thing?" or best of all, "What good will it do? It's just going to burn out again anyway!"

Finally, when I can stall no longer, and I do the job, I find not only that the bulb took all of two minutes to replace, but also that it really is nice to have the extra light. What's more, I don't even recognize the extra cost on the light bill.

Getting started with the practice of blessing your children is a little like replacing a light bulb. It really isn't much work when you actually do it, it doesn't take much time, and the results are better than you thought. But I can't give you a simple formula that says, "Do these five things and all your troubles will end—one size fits all."

You see, there's no right way or wrong way to bless your children. A blessing of any sort is still a *blessing*—something good and powerful and precious. I believe the only mistake you can make is to decide that for fear of doing something wrong you'll do nothing at all. A sincere, loving blessing that's poorly delivered is still infinitely better than no blessing at all.

Common Questions When Starting Out

Having said that, let's look at some of the common questions folks have when they want to get started blessing their children.

1. What age should my children be when I start, and how old should they be when I stop?

The answer to this one is simple. Just ask yourself, "At what age do I want them to begin receiving the benefits of being blessed, and how long do I want that to continue?"

It doesn't matter whether they're fifteen years old or just fifteen months, or whether or not they understand the words being spoken. The longer you wait to begin, the fewer opportunities you'll have to impart God's grace to them in this way.

The ideal time may no longer be available, but to take full advantage of the time that remains, start today. Communist leaders used to say, "Give us a child until he is five years old, and we will have him the rest of his life." Judging by what has happened to so many communist governments recently, they probably no longer believe that. But in some ways the premise is still true.

The overwhelming majority of all we will ever learn in life we learn before we start school. Of course, all is not lost if we missed that time in our children's lives. God can and will make up for lost time. But nothing can be gained by further delay.

By the same token, our children are never too old to be blessed. They need the favor and power of God in their lives, and always will. So why would we ever want to stop blessing them?

Most older kids I know who have been blessed since an early age don't consider it a childish ritual they outgrew once they reached adolescence or adulthood. On the contrary, they now cherish the blessing more than ever. So even if our children move far away from home, we can bless them daily long-distance in our private prayer times.

2. Is bedtime the only time of day to bless your children?

Absolutely not. We can be grateful that God is up and awake all the time, and He's always ready to bless, any moment of the day. Since it's God who actually does the blessing, any time is the right time.

We should note, however, that structure and consistency can be important, especially to young children. The key here is to think through your day and find the best time for your family. It may be bedtime, or it may be mealtime. It may even be when your children leave for school so they can launch out on the new day with a blessing still ringing in their ears.

In fact, the right time might be all three of these. I don't believe you can overdose a child with blessing. In our home, for example, short "The-Lord-bless-you-in-school-today" blessings punctuated our morning good-byes to our kids.

Bedtime worked best for us for our special time of blessing, because it gave us more uninterrupted time. We could take longer if we wished, and it also gave the kids a chance to reflect on the day's activities. We also wanted it to be the last words they heard at night.

So many times kids are shouted at and told, "Get in your room and stay there!" or "How many times have I told you to go to bed!" This negative speech stays in their minds as they wrestle with sleep, and sooner than later it comes back to the parent in defiance, disobedience, and a thousand other destructive ways.

If the best time for your family isn't immediately obvious, just experiment a bit. Tell your kids what you want to do and why, and that you aren't sure when the best time would be. If they're older, ask for their suggestions.

A Norwegian Blessing

When I was a child, dinner time was our family's special time together, and it provided just the right context for a family blessing. We were always together for this meal. We talked about the activities of the day, laughed a lot and enjoyed a good home-cooked meal. But the most significant part of that mealtime was the blessing and thanksgiving that surrounded it.

Since my Dad was born and reared in Norway, and my mother's parents came to America from Norway as young adults, many Norwegian customs came with them, along with the language itself. One of the first things we learned to say in Norwegian was the table blessing. Dad made sure we understood what it meant, as well as how to say it. It goes like this:

> *I Jesu Navn går vi til bords*
> *Å spise drikke på dit ord.*
> *Dig gud til ære, os til gavn,*
> *Så får vi mat i Jesu navn, Amen.*

In the English translation:

> *In Jesus' name we go to the table*
> *to eat and drink at Your request.*
> *God to honor, us to bless.*
> *We receive this food in Jesus' name, Amen.*

This table blessing was said before the meal. Then after everyone finished eating and before any of us could leave, Dad would say "thank You to Jesus" for the food we had just eaten. This tradition has been lost in my home, and I regret that. It showed us the heart of gratitude my parents had for God's blessing on their and their children's lives.

Although this Norwegian blessing was said before the meal, Dad also would pray his own very personal and specific blessing on each of us around the table before we could begin eating. And let me tell you, when Dad "asked the blessing," he didn't leave anything out. Sometimes these blessings were said in Norwegian, but usually in English, and always with tears of gratitude and love to God for His goodness.

The blessings that Dad gave at these meals helped shape the desires of our hearts to fit the desires of God's heart for us. Dad's blessings gave each of his three boys God's perspective on what was important in this life and what was not. He would often pray, for example, "God, if it be Your will, I would rather have these boys pass out tracts on skid row than be the President of the United States." That prayer has certainly been answered!

Often Dad would quote a blessing from the Bible as well, such as the first five verses of Psalm 103:

> *Bless the Lord, O my soul,*
> *And all that is within me, bless His holy name.*
> *Bless the Lord, O my soul,*
> *And forget none of His benefits;*
> *Who pardons all your iniquities;*
> *Who heals all your diseases;*
> *Who redeems your life from the pit;*
> *Who crowns you with lovingkindness and*
> *   compassion;*
> *Who satisfies your years with good things,*
> *So that your youth is renewed like the eagle (NASB).*

When Dad repeated these words and wept, as he so often did, his children couldn't fail to see in him a heart of intense gratitude for God's favor and power—a heart filled with blessing and a desire to bless. I deeply miss those times together, but I thank the Lord for the blessing of godly parents.

3. *Does the blessing have to be spoken daily?*

Again, there are no hard and fast rules; you should do what seems right for your family. A daily blessing obviously gives you more opportunities to bless your kids than one that is less regular, but some families (like the Straleys) prefer to reserve the blessing for more special occasions—for example, birthdays, weddings, anniversaries, major life transitions, or even times of crisis.

Still other families prefer to have a regular time of family blessing, but on a weekly basis. One family I know chose the Saturday evening meal as the beginning of their weekly "Sabbath" together. At the beginning of the meal, the mother lit a candle, which remained burning throughout the following twenty-four hours as a reminder that the day was given to worship and rest. Then the father sang a blessing on the family members. It was a simple melody he had written to go with the closing words of Psalm 128, which in an earlier verse talks about the blessing of sitting down to eat with a wife "like a fruitful vine" and "children like olive plants around the table" (v. 3):

The Lord bless you from Zion,
And may you see the prosperity of Jerusalem
All the days of your life.
Indeed, may you see your children's children.
Peace be upon Israel! (vv. 5–6, NASB)

With the terms "Zion," "Jerusalem," and "Israel" understood to represent God's people everywhere, the blessing communicated to the family the father's desire that they and their descendants would forever thrive in the kingdom of God.

4. How do I decide what to say?

Take a look at the list of blessings we suggest in the back of this book, as well as the blessings that begin each chapter. One of these might be best for your needs. Or try using a concordance to find all the occurrences of the word "bless" in the Bible; among them you'll find a number of blessings you can recite, and you'll learn a great deal as well about how blessings were given in biblical times. Of course, you always have the option of adapting one of the blessings you find, or of creating your own.

With all these possibilities, you shouldn't have any problem finding something meaningful to say when you bless your children. Your toughest problem will probably be choosing from among so many!

5. Does the blessing have to be the same every time?

Not at all. You and your family can vary the blessing however you see fit.

Of course, we should repeat that structure and consistency are important, especially for younger children. There is a certain value to saying the very same words over and over again every night of a child's growing-up years; it gives him or her a sense of stability, of predictableness, of security. In our family, for example, after all these years of saying the blessing from Numbers 6:24–26, no other words in my vocabulary could possibly carry the same impact or trigger the same lifetime of warm memories for my children as the words that begin: "The Lord bless you and keep you. . . ."

You certainly don't need to seek novelty for its own sake. But if you think a fresh form of the family blessing would benefit your children, why not try a different one? You can't go wrong. You might even want to learn a whole series of blessings and rotate them regularly. Or create your own.

In fact, the blessing doesn't have to have a set form at all. Like prayer, it can be spontaneous as well. It can even be sung!

You might want to try different blessings for different occasions, according to what seems most appropriate. In *Fiddler on the Roof,* the aged rabbi was asked whether or not there were a proper blessing for the Tsar of Russia—who, of course, had shown himself to be a deadly enemy to the Jewish people living in his empire. Convinced that *everything* in our lives has an appropriate blessing—even our enemies—the rabbi answered mischievously, "A blessing for the Tsar? Of course. May God bless and keep the Tsar—far away from us!"

6. Is the father the only family member who can give the blessing?

By no means! As Christians we're all called to bless and be a blessing. As I've noted, even in our family, where I assumed the primary responsibility to give the family blessing, my wife often joined me in it, and she spoke the blessing to the kids when I was absent. Some families always have both parents give the blessing together. And single-parent homes without a father present are in no way excluded from the blessing. Even our children have given the blessing to one another.

7. Does blessing your children take the place of prayer?

Definitely not. I believe there are three vital kinds of conversation with God that we share with our children. These three kinds of conversation are like strands woven together to form a single braid which is infinitely stronger than the individual strands. On this braid, I believe, hang all the other disciplines we desire to develop in our children's Christian lives. And though the three are similar, they serve very different purposes.

Prayer *for* our children is one strand—interceding for them as the family's priest, lifting them and their needs up to the throne of God.

Prayer *with* them is the second strand—introducing them to God, bringing them into our own conversations with God, modeling for them a healthy pattern of regular communication with our Father.

The third strand is the *blessing*. It complements and strengthens the other two, reflecting the goodness and power, the fatherly heart of the God we talk to when we pray for and with our children. Yet it cannot take the place of prayer.

Suggestions for Starting

When you decide to begin the practice of blessing your children, let me suggest a few guidelines:

1. If your children are old enough to understand, before you begin, explain to them what you're planning to do and why you believe it's important.

Children who are too young to understand won't need an explanation, but you can assure them that you're doing something good that God wants you to do, and that it won't hurt. Children who are old enough to understand at least something of what you're doing will be naturally curious. They'll be much more cooperative and appreciative if they know why you're doing what you're doing and why it's important. Be sure to answer any questions as well as you can, whatever the child's age.

A dear friend of mine from the publishing industry, Lee Gessner, was visiting with me one night. As the conversation developed and we began talking about our kids, I shared with him our practice of blessing them and how I felt it benefited them. He liked the idea, so he decided to begin blessing his three children, who were ten, eight, and four at the time.

Nearly a year later I saw Lee again, and he could hardly wait to tell me the news. "Guess what? I've been blessing my children ever since we were together last time. It's great! I went home, took each one in my arms individually, put my hand on the child's head, and gave the blessing from Numbers chapter 6."

Lee was grinning widely as he told his story. "You know," he observed, "each of the children responds differently when I bless them. One gets right into it. He snuggles up to me when I hold him and almost purrs in the process. The second one just receives it nonchalantly, as a normal part of what Dad does. But the little guy—he stands at attention. His arms are at his sides and he's stiff as a soldier. To him, this is important. This is God touching him, and he wants to be as good as he can."

The kids each had a slightly different understanding of what the blessing was all about. But the important point is that from the beginning each one had *some* understanding of what was going on that held meaning for him or her.

Lee still blesses his kids today, even though they're several years older. The biggest step was the first one, and the rest have come easy. Remember: Starting is the hardest part. Once you begin, keeping on is the fun part.

2. Hold your children in your arms when you bless them.

Gary Smalley and John Trent have an excellent chapter in their book *The Blessing* called "The First Element of the Blessing: Meaningful Touch." In it they chronicle the value of parents' touching their children, citing examples and teaching from a spiritual, psychological, and physical perspective.

Hugging has always been as much a part of my extended family as saying "hello" or "good-bye." We virtually never do one without the other. Whether those involved are parents, spouses, children, grandparents, brothers (I have no sisters), or in-laws, it makes no difference. Whenever we greet one another or leave, we hug.

In fact, I hug almost anybody—my boss, co-workers, friends, my kids' friends, strangers (but not many of them). And when I hug folks who aren't family members, I often hear them comment: "Oh, I really needed that."

One of my son's buddies, a hard-working, no-nonsense, super-jock type, came to our house some time ago, and I gave him a hug. When I let him go, he said, "I like coming to the Garborgs' house. They give *hugs* here." Now he gives me hugs on Sundays after church.

From reading the Bible we can conclude that the patriarchs knew the value of touching. Jesus knew the value of it as well. He took the little children up in His arms and held them when He blessed them. We should too. It's one way of telling children that we accept them as they are, and it opens the door for them to receive the blessing when we give it to them.

Carlton and Lisa are in college today, but I still hold them in my arms when I bless them. It's one of the most treasured times of my day, and of their day as well. Should God grant that I live to be eighty when my kids will be in their fifties, I'll still be holding them when I bless them.

At the same time it's important to note that some people feel uncomfortable "hugging" others. Perhaps their families were not especially affectionate physically or certain experiences in their lives have caused them to resist close contact of the sort I am describing here. That's OK. A hand on the shoulder or on the arm can be a meaningful substitute for "non-hugging" families. I'd still like to encourage you, however, to explore ways in which you might learn to experience the closeness that can only come through a more physical expression of your affections.

3. Place your hand or hands on the heads of your children when you bless them.

This action is also modeled to us by the patriarchs and Jesus. And no wonder—the gesture has great spiritual significance and symbolism connected with it.

The Bible teaches that the "laying on of hands" was used for consecrating people for service to God, imparting the Holy

Spirit, and praying for the sick to be healed. In the church today it's also used in the symbolic gestures of baptism, confirmation, and ordination.

Larry Lenning, in his book *Blessing in Mosque and Mission,* notes that in the biblical context

> . . . the act of laying on of hands was a sacred act through which the blessings of God were given. The hands of the blesser were not sacred. But through these human instruments, God bestowed His benediction, power, grace and mercy. . . . in the light of the Jewish background of the New Testament and the early Church and with the evidence of the New Testament itself, the laying on of hands was a sacred act through which God bestowed varied blessings.[1]

The symbolism of "covering" our children is important here. We depict to them through this gesture the protection and care with which God shields them.

When Larry Christenson first told us about the family blessing back in 1972, he mentioned how placing his hand on the heads of his four children was like blessing his congregation at church. Every Sunday at the close of the church service, he would lift his hand symbolically out over the heads of his parishioners as he gave them a benediction from Scripture. It sent them on their way with a picture of the divine covering of protection. And it gives a picture to our children as well.

4. Always include in your blessing an invocation of the name of God.

It's the name of the one true God that separates this blessing from all other blessings in the religions of the world. Many non-Christian cultures have forms of blessing similar in intent and wording to those of the Christian faith. What sets the Christian blessing apart as a divinely powerful experience is the invoking of the name of the true God. This is why the non-Christian world cannot fully understand the meaning of our blessing: They don't know or understand the name of our God.

Much has been written on the name of God and the power it carries. I would encourage you to find some of those writings in your church library or Christian bookstore so you can read about this subject yourself.

When we contemplate the sheer awesomeness of God and the infiniteness of His power, we can begin to understand what can happen at the mere mention of His name. And we can identify with David's feelings when he cried out to God in Psalm 103:1: "Bless the Lord, O my soul: and all that is within me, bless his holy *name*" (NASB, emphasis added).

The form of God's name you use is, of course, up to you, according to what is most meaningful to your family. Many Christians use the Church's ancient tradition of invoking God with the name of the holy Trinity: "In the name of the Father, and of the Son, and of the Holy Spirit." Others prefer simply "in Jesus' name." In either case, the powerful name of our Lord sets apart our blessing as a vessel of *His* grace.

5. Teach your children that even on days when you forget to give the blessing or are unable to give it for some reason, the blessing of God still rests on them and protects them, and that they can speak blessings on themselves.

Younger children especially learn to look forward so much to the comfort and security of the blessing that they may become unsettled if it's not given for some reason. In the chapter of kids' testimonies we presented, for example, some of the children remembered being afraid or unable to sleep if their parents didn't bless them on a particular night.

We want to avoid encouraging our kids to think that God's blessing, and especially His protection, comes *only* through the spoken words of a parent. If we emphasize to young ones that the family blessing is simply *one* of the *many* ways the Lord pours out His favor and power, and that they have the privilege of speaking blessing as well, then we can help them to feel more secure in God's love and in our own.

A Brief Review

Here's a brief review of the main points we've made in this chapter to help you get started:

- Start today, no matter how old your children are, and don't stop.

- Every night at bedtime is a good time to bless your kids, but by no means the only time. Find what works best for your family, with regard both to time of day and to frequency of the blessing.

- Choose your words for the blessing by referring to the suggestions in this book, finding them in the Scripture, or creating your own. The words don't necessarily have to be the same every time, though there are benefits to continuity.

- Blessing should never take the place of prayer. Blessing, prayer *for* your children, and prayer *with* your children are all important ways of including children in our conversations with God.

- Explain to your children what you're doing and why.

- Hold your children in your arms when you bless them, and place your hand or hands on their heads.

- Always invoke the name of God when you bless them.

- Teach your children that the family blessing is only one of the ways God uses to bless and protect us.

Above all, don't be afraid to start. Practice on your kids. It's okay! When doctors start in business they open a medical "practice." Lawyers open a legal "practice." And they practice on you and me. Now that's scary. But there's nothing scary about blessing. So start today—and God bless you when you do!

II

◇

People of Blessing

The God of love and peace shall be with you.
The grace of the Lord Jesus Christ, and the love of
God, and the fellowship of the Holy Spirit, be with you all.
2 Corinthians 13:11b, 14, NIV

8

◇

Speaking Well of Our Children

In Part One of this book we've focused on blessing in a specific sense: the kind of blessing we read about in the Bible in which one person intentionally and explicitly invokes the goodness of God into the life of another person through the spoken word. In Part Two we turn our attention to blessing in a more general sense. Here we'll consider in a broader context how the power of words operates in our daily lives to strengthen or to hurt those around us—not just within family relationships, but within all our relationships.

God is a God of blessing, we've said; the Bible makes that clear. But we must note how the Bible shows as well that God's people are to be a *people of blessing*. The Lord not only pours out His power and favor on us; He also appoints us to be a blessing, just as He did Abraham. He has delegated to us the role of conveying His grace to others, and one of the primary means by which we can do that is through the power of our daily words.

We Can Speak Life and Death

"Death and life," says the book of Proverbs, "are in the power of the tongue" (18:21, NASB). Nowhere is that reality clearer than in the dynamics of family life. The words parents speak to their children day in and day out, even in casual conversation, create an atmosphere in the home over time that either chokes and poisons their young spirits or nourishes and strengthens them. The results can be devastating or life-giving: "Reckless words

pierce like a sword, but the tongue of the wise brings healing"
(Proverbs 12:18, NIV).

We have the daily choice as parents to speak life or death to
our children. Speaking "death"—destroying their self-esteem
with negative labels, nicknames, household reputations, or self-
fulfilling prophecies—is what the Bible calls "cursing"; we will
deal with that issue specifically in chapter 10. But even if we
rarely inflict those kinds of verbal injuries on our children,
we may still be guilty of draining the life from their spirits by
our negligence or reluctance to "speak well" of them.

A Sin of Omission

I'm reminded of the young boy in Sunday school who was asked
by his teacher to tell the class the difference between "sins of
commission" and "sins of omission." He thought for a moment
and then declared, "Sins of commission are sins we have committed. Sins of omission are sins we were supposed to commit,
but never got around to."

That budding theologian didn't quite get it right, but at
least he had a firm grasp of the meaning of "omission": The
things we omit are usually the things we were supposed to do,
but never got around to.

How often do we commit the sin of omission when it comes
to praising our children and speaking well of them? Words that
encourage, empower, and build up—in short, words that *bless*
—somehow seem to get lost in the daily shuffle of telling our
kids to come to dinner, to brush their teeth, to finish their homework, to quit teasing their kid brother!

Frequently when someone has spoken kindly of another
person to me, I've gone to that other person and passed on the
comments. Almost without exception they give the same response: "Why, thank you. I really appreciate hearing that. I wish
they would tell me that themselves!" This happens almost everywhere—between bosses and their employees, between husbands
and wives, and especially between parents and their children.
For one reason or another, people fail to praise one another.

Speaking "Eulogies"

Just think about the English word for "speaking well" of some-one that comes from the Greek root *eulogeo*—"eulogy." When do people present eulogies? When the person being praised has died! Isn't it sad that we typically wait until people are gone and unable to hear our words before we eulogize them, before we "speak well of them" or "express praise" concerning them?

Proverbs 25:11 says, "A word fitly spoken is like apples of gold in settings of silver" (NKJV). An appropriate expression of appreciation is an adornment placed on the recipient that brings honor to the person whether he or she is alone or in the presence of others. And now is the best time to adorn our children with such blessings—not when it's too late for them to hear what we have to say.

Words of Respect

Nor is this general kind of blessing limited to words spoken *about* our children. It can also refer to the words we use when speaking *to* them. Words that show respect for them can elevate their self-esteem and their level of performance, and can trans-form their attitude about what they do.

Far too often, I've heard business managers give "com-mands" to their secretaries as though they were some sort of drill sergeant—rather than asking them politely to do something. Whenever workers are told "Do this!" or "Bring me that!" their morale and their productivity slide. If we only stopped to think what a difference could be made by prefacing our requests with a genuine "Would you mind" or "Could you please," we could honor our employees and coworkers and create a more joyful, efficient workplace. Then, when the job is finished, a "thank you" or "I appreciate what you did" would be an added blessing.

If these words are appropriate at work, they're even more appropriate at home with our spouse and children. Family blessings often take on the form of a kind word prefacing a request. Look at what Paul says in Ephesians 4:29: "When you talk, do not say harmful things. But say what people need—words that will help others become stronger. Then what you say will help those who listen to you."

These kind words can be said in private or in public. They will always be appreciated and will invariably come back to you in the form of changed behavior on the part of the recipient. That is, in fact, the very nature of blessing:

> Finally, all of you should live together in peace. Try to understand each other. Love each other as brothers. Be kind and humble. Do not do wrong to a person to pay him back for doing wrong to you. Or do not insult someone to pay him back for insulting you. But ask God to bless that person. Do this, because you yourself were called to receive a blessing (1 Peter 3:8–9).

Give, and You Will Receive

Of course, we should hasten to say that the reason we bless our children or anyone else by speaking well of them is not to control them or to squeeze a little more performance out of them. That motive will be recognized immediately as manipulation by the receiver of such a "blessing," and could well backfire on us. No, we bless people because it's the right thing to do! Period. Receiving a blessing in return is simply a bonus that God sends our way for obeying Him.

The same principle applies to giving of any sort, including our financial giving. Scripture says, "Give, and it will be given to you" (Luke 6:38, NASB), not "Give so that it will be given to you." If we give, we get back. But that can't be our motivation for giving. It's simply God's law.

If we give an insult, we will receive one in return, and usually in thirty minutes or less. What's worse, the relationship will usually be soured as well. On the other hand, if we give a kind word, a blessing, a "eulogy," we will most likely receive the same in return—and everyone involved will grow stronger in the process.

Words That Are Warranted and Sincere

In order for a blessing of this type (the kind word or expression of praise) to be received well, it must meet at least two conditions. First, it must be *warranted.* You may have to think hard to find a quality you can praise in someone—even, at times, your own child. But if you keep looking, you'll find it. An unwarranted blessing is an empty and hollow blessing. In fact, it's not really a blessing at all, and may have a negative result.

The second condition for a genuine blessing of this sort is that it must be *sincere.* An insincere compliment is easily detected, and it leaves a bitter taste in the mouth of both the giver and the receiver. But a sincere compliment does more to build the confidence of those around us than almost anything else we can do for them.

Graduation "Eulogies"

During the early spring of our son's senior year in high school, Mary and I were talking with the parents of some of his classmates. His school was a small Christian institution with a graduating class of only eleven. Several of these kids had actually been together since the fall when they'd started school a dozen years earlier. Needless to say, it was a closely knit group.

We were reflecting on how the parents of those kids formed a close group as well. Together we had watched them grow up. Four of the boys had been playing on the school's basketball, softball, and soccer teams together since the seventh grade. We had seen the character development that comes from teamwork and competition, as well as the honing of their skills in sports. We had also seen their growth as friends and in the Lord.

After all those years together, we couldn't really speak any more of "my kids" and "your kids"—they were all "our kids." The ten sets of parents with their eleven kids made one big family. And now our time together was drawing to a close as they finished their last season of basketball.

As we talked about the uniqueness of this class of eleven, a desire to do something special for them began to grow in our hearts. We decided we would have an "Appreciation Night." Though we looked forward to the event excitedly, I don't think any of us realized at the time how powerful the evening would be or the impact it would have on both parents and children.

Only the parents and their senior-class children were invited—no pastors, teachers, coaches, siblings, or other relatives. Some parents had to adjust their business schedules to be there. Some of the kids had to leave softball practice early that evening to get ready in time. For others, homework had to be postponed. It seemed that a sacrifice was made by almost everyone involved.

We sat at tables of six—two couples and their children at each table. The food was catered to allow us to focus on our children rather than on preparations. So the conversation over dinner was light and relaxed.

After the meal, we gathered around the fireplace to begin the program. There was laughter aplenty as we "roasted" each of the seniors. (Underclass students had been only too willing to give the juicy morsels we needed.)

Then the powerful part began.

One by one, each father of these eleven kids came up to the front of the room and, from the deepest part of his being, declared to his child, before the child's peers, those things that he most appreciated about his son or daughter. As they looked into each others' eyes, father and child wept. One dad prefaced his words with a confession: "I have never really told you this before. . . ."

Each father's list of comments was specific and individual, which made them much more meaningful than a simple "I appreciate you." Their "words fitly spoken" included golden treasures like these:

"You are the type of daughter, the type of person, who has helped me grow."

"You have a heart for God."

"God will reward you for all the hidden sacrifices you have made."

"My only regret is that I didn't have ten more just like you!"

"I see the treasures God has put in you beginning to blossom."

"I see Jesus in you."

These fathers' heartfelt remarks were "eulogies" in the best sense of the word—expressions of praise given before it was too late for the person being praised to hear them, expressions not heard often enough by people who deeply desired them. And their power to bless the children involved was intensified because these words were spoken by one of the most significant people in their young lives: their fathers.

At the end of each father's comments, his son or daughter came of his or her own accord and embraced him. The tears flowed freely in these tender moments as each "I love you" was exchanged. Then, to conclude, one senior's parent sang the blessing found in Numbers 6:24–26 (Aaron's blessing, quoted in the first chapter) to a tune her father had written himself.

No one was embarrassed by the intensity of emotion that night. In those words of family blessing, a dam had burst, allowing feelings of gratitude and encouragement to flow out—in some cases, perhaps, feelings that hadn't been expressed in years.

That "Appreciation Night" had such a profound impact on me that even now, almost three years later, just to recall and write about it has moved me deeply once more. Being a part of such a time of explicit family blessing has changed my life. It serves to remind me as nothing else could just how critical and powerful are a parent's words to a child.

Fathers, if you haven't been regularly blessing your children with kind words that come from a heart of gratitude, start today. If you haven't been speaking well of them and expressing praise to them, begin right away. It's not enough just to refrain from speaking negatively of them or to them.

You desire the best for your children, so take the initiative. Once you make an active commitment to bless your family daily, God will do His part.

May the Father, from whom his whole family in heaven and on earth derives its name,

out of his glorious riches strengthen you with power through his Spirit in your inner being,

so that Christ may dwell in your hearts through faith, that you, being rooted and established in love, may have power, together with all the saints, to grasp how wide and long and high and deep is the love of Christ, and to know this love that surpasses knowledge— that you may be filled to the measure of all the fullness of God.

adapted from Ephesians 3:14–19, NIV

9

◇

There Is Blessing in a Name

If the words we parents speak to our children have the power of life or death, then consider the phenomenal power resident in the one word we speak to them far more than any other—the word they will hear throughout their entire lives. I'm referring, of course, to a child's *name.*

A good name is a great blessing. A bad name is a curse. I'm reminded of a cartoon that once pictured a proud Puritan father of the colonial American period introducing his five daughters, who were all standing primly in line. The first four were beautiful; the last one looked as if she had just survived a cyclone. But the father's presentation of each by name explained the difference: "I want you to meet my children: Hope, Faith, Charity, Prudence, and *Pestilence.*"

In the biblical world, a person's name was inextricably bound up with the person's nature. The authority to give a name was seen in some sense as the authority to control the one named. Consequently, the giving of names was a serious affair. And it still is today, whether the name is a given name, a surname, a nickname, or a reputation.

Given Names Can Be a Blessing

Our name is undoubtedly one of our most treasured possessions. It's part of what distinguishes us from everyone else, and—as with the unfortunate girl in the cartoon we mentioned—in many ways it shapes who we become, for good or for ill. The first gift we parents give a child is his or her name, and it's a gift that will last an entire lifetime. Because of this significance, selecting a name for our children must be considered carefully. We can literally bless or curse our children with the name we give them.

The name that can most significantly serve as a vital form of constant blessing and encouragement to our children is their first or given name. Great thought and care should go into selecting these life-long labels; something that's merely "cute" or popular at the time may not be the best choice. (I know, for instance, of mothers who named their children after soap opera characters.) Most importantly, we should ask God to make clear His choice for our child's name.

Once we give them the name we believe is right, we can further bless our children by making certain that they know what their name means and why we chose it for them. Then, every time we call them by name, we're blessing them.

How Our Children Were Named

When I first went to Puerto Rico in early 1966, our mission had several Christian leaders come as guests. During the two weeks they were with us, I was tremendously impressed with the Christlike spirit I saw lived out in one of those men in particular. His name was Carlton Spencer. When he and the others left, I told the Lord that if I ever had a son, I would name him Carlton, because the deepest desire of my heart was that he, too, would be Christlike. Three years later, Mary and I got our son, and as I had told the Lord, we named him Carlton.

When our daughter came along three years later, we named her Lisa Faith. Lisa means "consecrated to God" because she has been consecrated to Him since before she was born. As for her second name, the meaning is clear. On various occasions when the subject of faith has come up, she has stated with delight, "My middle name is 'Faith.'"

Throughout both our children's lives we've reminded them of why we chose their particular names for them, at the same time letting them know our prayers and desires for them. In fact, since the time they were small, we've had hanging on our wall at home a plaque with each of our family members' names and its spiritual meaning.

Of course, if you're simply unable to decide among all the many names you like, you have two choices: You can either wait till you have more children to use the other names, or you can do as the parents of my mother's classmate did some eighty years ago. They decided to use all those good names on one child, naming her Heidi Dumpty Mandy Fitz Gusta Maria Matilda Jane Bugs! Can you imagine writing all that on a check?

God's Interest in Our Names

We find examples in the Bible of just how important the naming of a child can be to God. Jesus, for example, was given His name by God before He was born. It was a name the Father had carefully chosen, because it signified that He would be the Savior (Luke 1:31; 2:21).

When Jesus' cousin, John the Baptist, was born, we're told that his parents surprised the family and friends with a name that broke the tradition of naming a child after a relative. The Bible doesn't say, but it's likely that John's father, Zacharias, gave the boy the name "John" in obedience to God's specific instructions, because as soon as he did, his voice returned— ending a nine-month discipline God had imposed on him for disbelief (Luke 1:18–20, 59–64).

My friend Paul Thigpen and his wife, Leisa, found out that God had a choice for the names of their children as well. When Leisa was carrying their first child, they spent months looking through name books and debating the relative merits of scores of names. At last they decided on Matthew Zachary (meaning "God's gift" and "God remembers") for a boy and "Hannah Elise" ("grace" and "consecrated to God") for a girl.

Just a few weeks before the due date, Paul was in prayer and heard God saying to him that they had the wrong name for a girl. Instead, it was to be "Lydia Marie," a name he and Leisa had never discussed before. Paul was certain of what he had heard, but it had taken so long for the two of them to settle on a name that he was hard pressed to know how to raise the subject again. What if Leisa didn't like the name?

Finally, however, he said to Leisa: "Honey, as I was praying, I believe I heard God say that we have the wrong girl's name."

"I'm so relieved to hear you say that," she replied. "When I was praying, I heard the same thing. I believe the name God has picked out is one we've never talked about—Lydia Marie."

A few weeks later, Lydia Marie was born. In Scripture, the woman named Lydia, who helped Paul found the church at Philippi, was known as "a worshipper of God." Marie is the French form of Mary, who was called "the handmaiden of the Lord." These godly women have always been held up as Lydia's role models, and she is learning to follow their example.

The Thigpens' second child was named in the same way. He was due on Christmas Eve, so his parents had chosen the names "Gloria Joy" and "Gabriel Luke." But a few weeks before, God again spoke to Paul and Leisa independently, saying, "His name shall be Elijah John"—once more, two names they had not before considered. When the parents compared notes and found out that once again they had heard the same thing in prayer, they knew that the boy had been named.

One week before Christmas, Elijah John arrived—named for the two great prophets of the Old and New Testaments. No doubt God had an interest in the names chosen for him and for his sister. And every time their parents call their names, they are speaking to them the blessing of God.

Middle Names Are Important, Too

In the Bible we read of several people whose names changed, usually to signify some important change in their identity resulting from a life-changing encounter with God. Abram became Abraham (Genesis 17:5); Sarai became Sarah (v. 15); Jacob became Israel (Genesis 32:28); Solomon became Jedidiah (2 Samuel 12:24–25); Simon became Peter (Matthew 16:18); and Saul became Paul (Acts 13:9). In each case the new name was part of a blessing, a reception of God's power and favor into their lives.

Today some folks change their names as well, often for the same reason. One common way to change is to begin going by the middle name instead of the first name (or if the child is known by the middle name, to switch to the first). That happened with one of my friends, who at his conversion changed from using his first name, Thomas, to using his middle name, Paul. He decided that instead of being the "doubter" he would become a man of faith.

For this reason, it's important to make sure that both given names have a special significance. You never know whether your child might someday choose to go by a middle name.

The Blessing of the Surname

Surnames, or "last names" as we call them in the United States, tell much more about our kids than just where they sit in the classroom. Surnames declare our heritage. They carry with them the reputations of those who went before us—whether it was our grandfather who was known for bravery in the war, or our older brother who was known for harassing his schoolteachers! Surnames may also reveal our ancestors' occupation, our nationality, our race, or even our religion.

Though our last names can be a great blessing, some of us may wonder how. Consider my own name: Garborg. I remember that one day a friend of mine and his son saw me walking down the street, and the boy asked: "Who is that, Dad?"

"Rolf Garborg," his father replied.

"What?" said his son. "Why would anyone want to be called 'Rough Cardboard'?"

I'm not the only one to put up with teasing because of my name. I once knew of a dentist named Doctor Toothacher and another called Doctor Payne; a veterinarian named Doctor Slaughter; a Baptist missionary named Sprinkle; and a used car salesman named Joe Swindle. One of my friends is named Faith Matters—the only person I know whose name is a sentence.

In my grade school class of twenty-four kids, there were three who were constantly teased for having the last names Knear (pronounced "near"), Farr, and Close. I even knew two Mennonite missionaries working together in Puerto Rico whose last names were Nestley and Hershey!

A Link to Our Heritage

Despite the fun folks may have with some of our surnames, these titles form important links to our heritage. Knowing something about our ancestors can be a useful way of filling our surname with special meaning for our children, thus making the name a blessing. Research into our family tree might even help us find ancestors whose character, behavior, or vocation can serve as role models for our children.

If we look back at our own family history, we may see continuity not only in occupation or trade, but also in character. Scripture assures us that "the sins of the fathers" are visited "upon the third and fourth generations" (Exodus 20:5), and we might note from experience that the same is often true of the blessings as well. Some studies of family trees reveal a remarkable string of criminals spanning many generations. Others have shown a similar line of statesmen, clergy, or educators.

Of course, we should emphasize to our children that we can choose which of these character examples in our past we will perpetuate. If necessary, we can even pray to break any curses that may have hung over our family for years. It's up to us whether our descendants after us will be able to point with legitimate pride to our example and claim a godly heritage for themselves—embodied in the blessing of an honored surname.

The Meaning of a Surname

If you do some research into the literal meaning of your surname —or even into its historical associations—you may discover some special significance in it that will make it a further blessing for your children. The spiritual significance of a surname like

"Christian" or "Bishop" is obvious. But even with an unusual name like my own, hidden meanings can be surprising.

My two brothers and I have long been involved in the distribution of Christian literature. At one time, my older brother, Loren, was the director of literature missions of Bethany Fellowship for Central and South America and the Caribbean, while my younger brother, Kent, and I were in charge of the international division of Zondervan Publishing House. Kent covered Europe and Africa; I covered Asia and the South Pacific, and we shared Canada. Among the three of us, we literally covered the globe with Christian literature.

On one of Kent's trips he passed through the Orient. While in Hong Kong, he noticed a file with the name "Garborg" on it. Next to it were two Chinese characters. He found out from a Chinese clerk that those were the two characters for the name "Garborg" written in Chinese. He asked if those marks were just a transliteration of the sounds of our name, or if they had actual meaning.

"Oh, they have actual meaning," said the clerk. "This one is how we write 'gar,' and it means 'to spread,' while this one is 'borg,' which means 'abroad' or 'over a wide area.'"

Was it simple coincidence that when all of us were working abroad in the distribution of Christian literature we discovered the meaning of our name in Chinese to be "to spread abroad"— or can there be more significance to our surnames than we realize? In either case, it was a great blessing to these three brothers to realize that every time someone called us "Garborg," he was naming the vocation God had given us.

The Blessing of a Good Reputation

Another meaning of the word "name" is *reputation*. "A good name," the Bible says, "is more desirable than great riches; to be esteemed is better than silver or gold" (Proverbs 22:1, NIV). A good reputation is one of the greatest blessings our children can carry.

Earning a "good name" begins during childhood. Teachers

not only observe the work that our children do, but also the character qualities they exhibit, such as positive attitude, proper response to authority, setting and reaching goals, school spirit, neatness, and getting along with others. Whenever Carlton and Lisa brought home their report cards, the first place I looked was on the back of the card where these observations about character appeared. They were infinitely more important to me than my children's grades. And when we had parent-teacher meetings, the discussion focused not on their grades, but on their behavior.

The importance of developing this type of "good name" was exemplified in our kids' school during their spring awards night. (Since the name of their school was Bethany Academy, this annual event was naturally called "The Academy Awards"!) Appropriate and genuine recognition for academic achievement were always expressed by the teachers and the principal, but the highest honors were all tied to the winning student's character, integrity, school spirit, unselfishness, and willingness to strive for excellence.

The blessing of a good reputation for our children is obvious. It goes before them and opens doors of opportunity for them. It becomes their servant, and if they treat that servant well and don't abuse it, it will stay with them their whole lives.

Timothy, the apostle Paul's trusted companion, had that type of reputation. When Paul learned of the need in the Philippian church, he wrote:

> I hope in the Lord Jesus to send Timothy to you soon. I will be happy to learn how you are. I have no other person like Timothy. He truly cares for you. Other people are interested only in their own lives. They are not interested in the work of Christ Jesus. You know the kind of person Timothy is. You know that he has served with me in telling the Good News, as a son serves his father (Philippians 2:19–22).

What parent wouldn't want to have a son or daughter carry the life-long blessing of that kind of reputation?

We're all responsible and accountable for our own reputation. But we can also influence others in the reputation they earn. As parents we have the greatest opportunity and obligation to do just that. We should be sobered to realize that if we don't choose to be a positive influence on our children in the development of their "name" in this regard, we will by default be a negative influence.

A "Household Reputation"

Even within the four walls of our own home, a child can develop a reputation that serves to bless or curse. Most families probably recognize what we might call a "household reputation" among family members that labels a child in one way or another: "Well, Jill's just lazy"; "You know Gary—he never gives up"; "George will eat whatever doesn't eat him first."

When my family and I moved back to Minneapolis from Puerto Rico, the transition was an emotionally disruptive time for us all. Everything was turned upside-down, especially for our kids, and worst of all for Lisa—who was just three at the time. She missed her playmates and the surroundings she had in Puerto Rico, and she began to change from an energetic, buoyant, happy little girl into a whining, fussy, demanding one.

I wasn't dealing with her changes very well and soon found myself giving her negative reinforcement that only made matters worse. She was getting on my nerves, and even though I continued to bless her at night, I was counteracting those blessings with the negative responses I was giving her at other times of the day.

About that time my brother Kent gave me a book called *See You at the Top* by Zig Ziglar. One story that Zig told was especially appropriate to our struggle with Lisa's emotional change. He told how his second daughter, Cindy, changed from being a whiner to being a happy child through the power of a positive reputation at home.

Cindy (at the time the middle child) had been saddled with expectations that she would be different in a negative way from her older and younger siblings. She responded to the expectations accordingly. So her father often said, "Why does Cindy whine so much? Why isn't she happier and more cheerful?"

When the Ziglars realized they were building a poor reputation in the family for Cindy, they began making an intentional change in the way they referred to her. Instead of "cursing" her with the reputation of a whiner, they began calling her "the little girl everybody loves because she is so happy."

The result? Cindy became a different child. She even changed her own nickname from "Tadpole" to "Happy Tadpole."[1]

After reading that story, I began to practice this same approach on Lisa, reaffirming those qualities we knew she had. Now, whenever I saw her I said, "How is my happy little girl who smiles all the time?" Amazingly, within a matter of days the fussing and whining ceased and a broad smile appeared on her face again. She had been blessed by the new reputation she was given and began to live up to it. And she still does some fifteen years later.

The Blessing of a Nickname

Somewhat related to a person's reputation is a person's nickname. If you doubt that even a nickname can be a blessing or a curse, simply ask yourself: Which nickname would you prefer to have follow you throughout your life and beyond—"Alexander the Great" or "Ivan the Terrible"?

Most nicknames are verbal caricatures, which take a dominant feature, trait, action, or skill and blow it out of proportion. The problem with most of them is not so much that they're distorted, but rather that they exclude all other attributes or characteristics. No doubt Thomas had many strong points, but he is known as the doubter. In the same way, Alexander was likely not "great" in every way.

At their worst, nicknames are intended either to intimidate or to put down; the cruelest of all are tied to race, physical appearance, or handicap. No wonder the literary critic William

Hazlitt once said, "A nickname is the heaviest stone that the devil can throw at a man."

Other nicknames, however, are based on positive character qualities: "Champ," "Sparkle," "Cutie." They can be a source of encouragement and affirmation, especially when parents use them to bless their children. Still other nicknames are meant as "pet" names or terms of endearment: "Sugar Bear," "Cookie," "Sunshine." These too can be a blessing as they signal to children their parent's affection and the special place they hold in the parent's heart.

Even Jesus gave nicknames to some of His disciples. To wavering, impulsive Simon, for example, He gave the nickname "Rock" (Peter) as a way of affirming His confidence that Simon would indeed become firm in his character and his faith. No doubt that label made Peter want to live up to his name.

If you choose to use nicknames with your children, or with anyone else, for that matter, look for the positive, praiseworthy qualities that you want to cultivate in them. Give them names that will bless your children when you speak to them, names that show value and approval, names that build up instead of tear down.

Speak Blessing Through Your Family's Names

Ultimately, of course, the particulars of one's name are much less important than the fact that they're written in God's book of life (Revelation 21:15). Nevertheless, the names our children bear—whether their given names, surnames, nicknames, or reputations—can be for them a source of great blessing. Since words have such an impact on who our children become, and names have perhaps the greatest impact of all, we can bring God's grace into their lives by speaking over them names of blessing, and by helping them discover a blessing in the meaning of the names they have.

The Lord watches over you—
　　the Lord is your shade at your right hand;
the sun will not harm you by day,
　　nor the moon by night.
The Lord will keep you from all harm;
　　he will watch over your life;
the Lord will watch over your coming and going
　　both now and forevermore.

Psalm 121:5–8, NIV

10

◇

Breaking Curses

For many years I've had my office in our home. The house sits just high enough on a small knoll to give me a clear view of the roofs and tree tops that extend for a couple of miles to the northwest. It's a quiet and peaceful place to work most of the time.

Butting up against our lot line, however, is a small city play field, complete with an outdoor basketball court and an elaborate, wooden jungle gym. So during the summer months when the weather is warm enough here in Minnesota to have the windows open and the kids are out of school, the music of their laughter, squeals of delight, and screams of excitement invade the peace and quiet of my office.

As I listen to their words, I hear words of encouragement ("Come on! You can do it. Just try!"); challenge ("I bet you can't catch me! I dare you to jump from there!"); pleading ("Please, Mom, can't we stay a little longer?"); and enthusiasm ("That was fun! Let's do it again!").

But I also hear words of destruction—words of cursing. Most of these profanities come from teens, but some little kids, ages seven or eight, also use unbelievably foul language. At times literally every sentence I hear is filled with vulgar obscenities. And almost always these comments are directed toward some other child on the playground, ending with the recipient being shoved and left in tears.

For some it may be easy to think, *Oh, they're just kids letting off steam.* But more than likely, what they're really doing is mirroring what they've learned at home. Their behavior probably says more about their parents and home life than it does about them. It declares to all in earshot that these are kids who not only have failed to receive a blessing from their parents—they've evidently been cursed by them as well.

What Is a Curse?

As a boy, I used to think of "cursing" as using any of a long list of off-limits words. These words ranged from what we euphemistically called "mild oaths" to vulgarities, profanities, obscenities, and "taking the Lord's name in vain" (the worst of all). If any of these taboo terms were used, a discipline or punishment was administered, corresponding to the gravity of the offense.

A "mild oath" would get a mild "we don't speak that way in this house." "Dirty words" were washed out of our mouths with soap. I experienced this kind of "cleansing" first hand, and I can tell you that regardless of the chemical effects of the ingredients in the soap on the body (if any), the effect of the taste (which seemed to last for days—especially if a chunk of it got stuck to the inside of your teeth) tended to prevent further use of those words, at least in the presence of your parents.

I'm grateful that I never found out the punishment for taking God's name in vain. I was too terrified of the consequences to try that one.

Of course, we kids found two "safe" ways to use these off-limit words, but you could only use each approach once per bad word. They were either to ask, "What does _____ mean?" or to rush into the house after school and declare, "Mom, do you know what Billy said today? He said _____!" The sense of satisfaction was almost the same as having said these words yourself, but you escaped the punishment.

Such expletives—the kind I hear now on the playground—are the most obvious kind of curse a parent could speak to a child. But even those of us who would never use such language might be guilty of "cursing" our children in other ways.

Webster defines a curse as "a calling on God or the gods to send evil or injury down on some person or thing; to damn." In this sense, the blessing is the opposite of the curse, which calls down God's grace on a person or thing. So we shouldn't be surprised that just as our day-to-day speech to our children can bless them with encouragement, it can have the power to curse them as well. Even though most of us as Christians would never deliberately curse our children or friends, it can happen in many subtle ways, both by default and through ignorance of the effects of our behavior.

What the Bible Says about Curses

We find a broad range of meanings for the more than one hundred uses of the words for "curse" in Scripture. Some curses were verbal, some physical; some unintentional, others deliberate. Some were merely insulting, while others were outright damning. But all the biblical curses had one thing in common: They contributed toward the destruction of the person or object being cursed.

One particular biblical word for "curse," of interest to Christian parents, is the Greek word *kakologeo*. It's the opposite of *eulogeo*, the word for "bless" we looked at before which means literally "to speak well of, to express praise." Thus *kakologeo* means "to speak ill of, to revile."

Just as "speaking well" of our children is a blessing, "speaking ill" of our children is a curse. This is the "death" part of the biblical proverb cited before: "Death and life are in the power of the tongue" (Proverbs 18:21, NASB). Just as positive words have the power to convey God's grace, negative words have the power to destroy (Proverbs 12:18).

I read a quote recently that said, "Those who say, 'That's the way the ball bounces,' are usually the ones who dropped it." I think we can also safely say that those who cry, "Sticks and stones may break my bones, but words can never hurt me," are likely smarting from a freshly spoken "curse."

Actually, this type of curse has a real power to produce negative, destructive, even damning effects just as the blessing has a real power to produce positive, constructive, liberating effects. When we realize the harm done through this type of curse, we can see the need to replace it with words of blessing.

At the same time we might be sobered to realize that the curse injures not only the one who receives it; it hurts the one who speaks it as well. Even mildly negative words, when they become a pattern, work their way down into our spirits to do damage, in accordance with the biblical principle that whatever we sow, we'll also reap (Galatians 6:7–8). King David observed this principle in the case of one of his persecutors:

> He also loved cursing, so it came to him; and he did not delight in blessing, so it was far from him. But he clothed himself with cursing as with his garment, and it entered into his inward parts like water, and like oil into his bones (Psalm 109:17–18, NASB marginal note).

Considering the grave consequences of the curse, we do well to search our own patterns of speech with our children to identify and root out the negative words that might be found there. We can start with a look at the negative label.

The Negative Label

Jesus recognized the power of the curse—even the negative words that seem comparatively mild—when He observed: "Anyone who says to his brother, 'Raca,' is answerable to the Sanhedrin. But anyone who says, 'You fool!' will be in danger of the fire of hell" (Matthew 5:22b, NIV).

The word "raca" meant, loosely translated, "blockhead." If we take this scripture to heart, we must ask ourselves how many of us have ever given a child a negative label that was some version of "raca." We may laugh at the way Lucy calls Charlie Brown "blockhead" in the *Peanuts* comic strip; but her word is actually a curse. Coming from the lips of a parent, it can devastate a child.

I know one family where the words "fool," "dummy," "stupid," and "idiot" have been outlawed. Using them results in the same discipline that would be administered if one of those vulgar playground expletives were used.

The reason? The mother of this family constantly heard those very words when she was growing up, usually applied to her by her father—until she finally began applying them to herself. Because of the devastation they brought to her life, in her mind those hurtful labels are nothing short of obscene.

Only after years of being affirmed as an intelligent person by her husband and friends has this woman been able to free herself of the curse embodied in the word "fool." Is it any wonder Jesus threatened hellfire for folks who spoke that way?

What labels are we applying to our children? What messages are we giving them, not only about their intelligence, but about their character, their competence, and their physical appearance? When we apply descriptive words to them, are we cursing them or blessing them?

The Negative Nickname

The nickname is another kind of label that can bless or curse our kids. Though our intention may be to show affection, we must be careful. Through our "terms of endearment" we may be saddling them with a less-than-complimentary self-image or an unfair focus on one negative characteristic.

Think a minute: Would any self-respecting little boy really want to be called "Chubby"? Or consider the case of one family I heard about who called their preschooler "Puddin' Head." The nickname brought smiles from friends who thought it was cute, but what were those parents telling that child about their estimation of her intelligence? Is "Puddin' Head" really all that different from "Blockhead"?

We need to be aware of nicknames that our children may receive from others as well, especially from older siblings. I heard about one young man who was cursed this way by his older brother when he was in junior high and the brother was in high school. The older boy worked out in the gym and had a well-developed physique; the younger boy was late to enter adolescence and still quite skinny. So the older brother nicknamed him "Child Chest."

Years later, long after the older brother had given up on pumping iron and had grown quite overweight, the younger brother was still laboring under that curse. He exercised furiously, constantly measuring his chest; and though he had developed a handsome physique, in his own eyes his chest was never quite big enough.

The Negative Reputation

In an earlier chapter we mentioned the notion of a "household reputation," and it should be obvious how such a reputation can curse a child if it's negative. Zig Ziglar's story about telling everyone that his middle child was a whiner is a classic example of the problem (just as his change of the nickname was a classic example of the solution).

This kind of curse may take the form of negative *expectations* of a child. Negative expectations usually develop when our child has "failed" at something or has just not "measured up." We may tend to assume that the failure is somehow permanent or typical.

Such expectations may often be expressed in self-fulfilling prophecies like "You'll never amount to anything in life!" Sometimes they take the form of a rhetorical question like "Can't you do anything right?" Or we may even leave children on their own to fill in the blanks about our estimation of them: "Just who do you think you *are*, young man?"

Negative Comparisons

How many times have you heard yourself say something like this to your child: "Why did you do that, Sally? That little Anderson girl would never do anything like that." "John, why can't you be more like your brother Bobby?"

When I was just a youngster in grade school one of my

teachers tried to motivate me with this type of negative comparison. She would say repeatedly, "Now, Rolf, you can do better than that. Remember how well your older brother did when he was in this class!"

We usually mean well by these types of comments, but they're seldom received that way by the children. Typically, the recipients are always on the "short end" of the comparison and feel like failures when they hear them. They lose heart and tend to try even less to be as good as the one to whom they've been compared. This feeling becomes a curse that can stay with a person throughout an entire lifetime unless it's broken.

Often, when people—who've received these types of "curses" as children—grow up, they become underachievers. In fact, we often say of these people that they're "their own worst enemy," that they've "self-destructed" just before they could have achieved. Little wonder. They've been convinced since they were young that they weren't as good as the next kid.

As a child I felt this way to a great degree because what my teacher intended as a motivation, I received as an insurmountable obstacle—and I gave up trying. I felt that I could never do what my brother did (or more accurately, what my teacher implied that my brother did) in his academic achievements, and so I settled for mediocrity instead. My report cards often carried the disgraceful words, "Rolf does not work up to his ability." And I remember thinking, *What do they know about my ability?*

I felt like the "Charlie Brown" of our school. When I graduated from high school in 1961 in a class of 527 kids, there were 263 kids with a grade point average higher than mine and 263 with one lower than mine. You just couldn't get any more mediocre than that!

I knew I was loved and approved at home, but the "baggage" of mediocrity, this "curse" that I received in school, overshadowed the reinforcement I got at home. Even though I was reared in a warm Christian environment and went to church three times a week, it wasn't until I had a personal, public encounter with Jesus Christ as my Redeemer at the age of fifteen that this curse began to be broken.

When I knew for a fact that I was accepted by God, I began to accept myself as His creation—a creation He had said was "very good" (Genesis 1:31). Not mediocre! So I began to see those areas of strength I had, the gifts that God could use, and I stopped comparing my gifts to those of others.

I even began to hear things differently. Remarks I had previously received as put-downs now sounded more like compliments.

God even brought new friends into my life, friends who would build on the new foundation He had laid. I was still the same gangly, clumsy, immature kid I had been earlier, but these new friends saw the potential and began to draw it out of me. In particular, Nelson Clair, the youth pastor in our new church, took a special interest in Kent and me.

Nels, as we called him, believed in me and showed it by spending time with me and teaching me. He challenged me to be all I could be in Jesus. I'll be forever grateful for the way his attitude of blessing helped to break the power of the curse I had accepted as a child.

No Mixed Messages

All these kinds of curses, usually uttered when we're irritated or disappointed, give our kids the message that we don't believe in them. Sadly enough, if we don't make an intentional effort as parents to break such curses, they'll live under the shadow of them with two options: Someday they can themselves learn how to break the curses and remove them with a blessing; or they can attempt to escape the curses by having little or nothing to do with us.

As parents we have the opportunity to lift the expectations of our children and then shore them up with affirmations and blessings, or to torpedo the ambitions, talents, goals, and dreams of our kids by attacking them with curses. The good news is that we can choose which we will do.

The apostle James tells us, "We use our tongues to praise our Lord and Father, but then we curse people. And God made them like himself. Praises and curses come from the same mouth! My brothers, this should not happen" (James 3:9–10).

If we have made a conscious decision to speak a blessing on our children each day, then we also need to make a conscious effort to avoid cursing them. Otherwise we can inadvertently destroy much of the good God does through our blessing. We'll be sending mixed signals—and mixed signals are usually received for their *negative* value. As the apostle Paul asks, "Do you not know that a little leaven leavens the whole lump? Therefore purge out the old leaven that you may be a new lump . . ." (1 Corinthians 5:6, NKJV).

I know what I'm talking about when I refer to these kinds of curses; sad to say, I've spoken them to my kids myself. And whenever I have, I've invariably felt rotten about it. I knew that I really didn't mean what I said—it just kind of "came out." But the damage was done.

This is one situation where the great benefit of regularly blessing our children has been clear. Whenever I spoke wrongly to my children, I couldn't put them to bed and bless them without first making things right.

The Blessing As a Balm

In the ebb and flow of our busy lives today, we constantly encounter situations with other family members or fellow workers in which someone gets hurt. It may be a harsh remark, a thoughtless deed, a "stab in the back," a condescending look, or a simple failure to acknowledge someone. These and countless other emotional "cuts and scratches" are just part of daily life. They happen no matter how spiritual we are.

Ultimately, it isn't the fact that these abrasions occur which creates hard feelings and strained relationships. Rather, it's what we choose to do about them once they happen that makes them either a blessing or a curse.

I once knew a preacher, for example, who delighted in being confrontational. One day after a particularly sensitive parishioner complained of his crusty nature, he simply looked at her and replied, "Lady, if I'm rubbing your fur the wrong way, turn around." Needless to say, with that kind of response the emotional "scratch" she had received wasn't healed—in fact, it became infected.

At a recent large Christian convention, I made an innocent mistake. I had misunderstood the role of one of our company's female employees. I asked her if she would mind making copies of some materials to give to the account I was with at the time. She agreed, and within a few minutes was back with the requested copies.

I was grateful. The account was grateful. But the co-worker was upset that I had asked her to do a clerical chore for me.

She apparently told another female co-worker of the incident. Meanwhile, my next appointment was going a bit long and I needed to get a message to my boss about a change of schedule. So I asked the second worker if she would please call him and make the change. She said, "I could, but I won't. You've already used her—"she nodded to the first worker—"as a secretary once today." End of conversation.

I knew immediately that I had offended the first person. At first I thought, *How petty can you get?* But then I realized I was the offender, and if this was to go away it was up to me to make atonement. When the first woman returned, I went to her and apologized, telling her that I hadn't clearly understood her role.

She smiled and said, "Oh, that's okay! I was happy to do it." Then later in the week she thanked me. I knew then that we had an even stronger friendship.

With our kids the potential for offenses is enormous. It might be as simple as not giving them the time they need, or barking a "Can't you see I'm busy?" at them. Sometimes a slow response from our kids to do a task we've given them evokes an "If you know what's good for you, you'll be here in thirty seconds." These and other bumps and bruises build up during the course of a day, and unless they're dealt with when they happen, they'll be there when the kids go to bed. Worse yet, the children may be sent to bed as punishment.

Because our family had a fixed time for blessing our kids all those years, neither they nor we could go to bed angry. We just couldn't bless our children while we had a bad attitude toward them. We couldn't send them to bed without supper and then go in to bless them without making things right between us.

Can you imagine? You're angry with your son, so you send him to bed. Later, still angry, you go into his room, sit on the edge of his bed, give him a hug, put your hand on his head and say, "The Lord bless you and keep you (you disobedient little wretch), the Lord make His face shine upon you and be gracious unto you (even though what you really deserve is a swift kick in the britches), the Lord lift up His countenance upon you and give you peace (because you sure as shootin' won't get it from me). In the name of the Father, and of the Son and of the Holy Spirit, Amen."

No way. Can't do it. Won't work. If you make a firm commitment to bless your children at bedtime, you'll find it displaces the anger. It will be like a soothing ointment, a healing balm that dispels the hostilities of the day and allows both the offender and the offended to sleep in peace. I believe this is one way to obey the apostle Paul's command: "In your anger do not sin. Do not let the sun go down while you are still angry, and do not give the devil a foothold" (Ephesians 4:26, NIV).

Breaking the Power of Curses

Breaking the power of the curse in our family requires two steps: First, we must break any curses we're still under ourselves from our own childhood; and second, we must break the power of negative words we may have spoken over our children.

Often the curses spoken over us years ago will reappear in our home today as the "sins of the fathers" are "visited" upon subsequent generations. Just as children who were sexually abused are more likely to grow up to become abusers themselves, children who were called "idiot," for example, are more likely to pass on that curse to their own children. If that's the case with us, we must take the attitude that with our generation, "the buck stops here."

Getting Free of Our Own Curses

If you're laboring under the weight of one of the kinds of curses we've described, the following insights may help. They aren't meant to be a formula as much as they are a pattern. Because He made us to be individuals with free wills, God works with each one of us in a different way. So I'm leery of the "one-size-fits-all, five-easy-steps-to-spiritual-maturity-or-your-money-back" approaches to the victorious Christian life. But perhaps these points, along with some good counsel from your pastor, can help you to live free of the curses from your past:

1. Admit your need. Denial only serves to cement the problem further and perpetuate its effects. Just as the Holy Spirit came to convict the world of sin, He also came to convict it of judgment (John 16:8). Curses are judgments other people have put on us, whether deliberately or unwittingly. Acknowledge that you've been judged, and the Holy Spirit can begin to free you.

2. Identify as specifically as you can the nature of the curses spoken over you. Do you labor under the feeling that you just can't measure up? Then search your heart and your memory for curses that may have compared you unfavorably to a sibling or someone else. Do you struggle with the image of yourself as an unintelligent person? Consider whether one of your parents might have frequently called you "dummy" or "idiot" or some similar term when you were growing up. Are you unable to get motivated in your career? Perhaps as a child you were given the self-fulfilling prophecy, "You'll never amount to anything."

If you can identify the specific curses, write them down. You may have had many.

3. Recognize that through His death and resurrection, Christ has set us free from the power and effects of the curses of the enemy. That biblical promise (Galatians 3:13; Revelation 22:3) shows us that if we're carrying around a curse, we're carrying around baggage that's both unnecessary and defeating.

When the writer of Hebrews spoke of the need to "throw off everything that hinders" (Hebrews 12:1, NIV), he included the hindrances of these curses we carry needlessly.

4. *Pray aloud by name for each curse to be broken.* For example, if you had the "dummy" curse spoken over you, pray, "Father, in Jesus' name, I ask You now to break this curse over me. I renounce it—I will no longer submit to that judgment against me. I am not a dummy. I have a good mind that You gave me when You created me. So in place of this curse, I receive now from you the blessing You have given me."

Go through each curse in your list this way. After you pray to break each one, cross it out!

5. *Focus your attention on the blessing given us in Jesus— on what He has done for you, who you are in Him, and who you can become because of Him.* After telling us to cast off hindrances, the writer of Hebrews goes on to say:

> Let us fix our eyes on Jesus, the author and perfecter of our faith, who for the joy set before him, endured the cross, scorning its shame, and sat down at the right hand of the throne of God. Consider him who endured such opposition from sinful men, so that you will not grow weary and lose heart (Hebrews 12:2–3, NIV).

The power of sin and death is broken. The power of the curses we have carried is broken. We need only focus on Jesus and avail ourselves of His completed work. "Ask and it will be given you" (Matthew 7:7, NIV).

6. *Forgive those who put the curses on you.* Forgiving those who have hurt us is one of the most difficult things we'll ever be called on to do. This is especially true when the person who has caused us harm has not repented or shown any sign of remorse.

Nevertheless, it helps to remember the apostle Paul's words to the Colossians: "Forgive as the Lord forgave you" (Colossians 3:13, NIV). If we have received such a great forgiveness from God, do we dare not forgive others?

Jesus' parable of the ungrateful servant paints a graphic picture of what happens to us spiritually when we fail to forgive our fellow human beings: We end up in a spiritual prison with the "torturers" (Matthew 18:21–35, NASB). The surest way to remain under the curse of another person is to refuse to forgive that person.

When young Joseph in the Old Testament was stripped of his beautiful robe, thrown by his brothers into a cistern in the desert, and then sold as a slave for about eight ounces of silver, he could easily have harbored unforgiveness toward them. But instead he took an attitude of trust in God's providence: "You meant to hurt me," he told them. "But God turned evil into good. It was to save the lives of many people. And it is being done" (Genesis 50:20).

If we learn to forgive as Joseph did, trusting that God is in control, we can break the curse and walk in freedom.

7. *Replace the curse with blessing, praise, and the Word of God.* The apostle Paul told the Romans: "Do not be overcome by evil, but overcome evil with good" (Romans 12:21, NIV). You can overcome evil with good in at least three ways.

The first is by *blessing.* Once you've forgiven those who cursed you, bless them. Speak God's power and favor on them. This is the instruction given by Paul to the Romans: "Bless those who persecute you; bless and do not curse. . . . Do not repay anyone evil for evil" (Romans 12: 14, 17a, NIV). The strongest "repellent" for a curse is a blessing.

The second way to overcome evil with good is by *praise.* When you praise God for who He is, what He's done, and who He has made you to be in Christ, you overcome the evil of the curse. One of God's mightiest weapons is praise. He inhabits our praises (Psalm 22:3), and where God is, there is victory. So praise Him!

The third way to overcome evil with good is by the *Word of God,* which is "the sword of the Spirit" (Ephesians 6:17). Memorize and repeat often the scriptures that tell you who you are in Jesus. In fact, when you "take off" the curse someone has placed on you, you should "put on" not just the sword, but the *whole* armor of God listed in Ephesians 6:10–18.

Breaking the Curses over Our Children

Once we've begun to walk free of the curses spoken over us, we'll be free to break the curses over our children. The process is primarily the same—we must help our children through the same steps we've taken ourselves.

If the child is small, we'll have to pray to break the curses for them. We'll have to explain what Jesus has done for them in terms they can understand. And whatever age they are, we'll have to help them cultivate a pattern of blessing, praise, and memorizing Scripture to overcome the evil with good.

With some curses such as nicknames, we can replace the curse with a blessing by giving the person a new name. The young man who was dubbed "Child Chest" by his brother, for example, prayed with his pastor to break that curse. Then the pastor took the process a step further: He gave him a new nickname. "You're no longer 'Child Chest,'" he said. "Now your name is 'Champ Chest.'"

Recognizing Our Part in the Injury

The most important part of breaking our children's curses, however, is to recognize those that we ourselves have spoken. As parents we must search our hearts and memories to discover what words we might have spoken that need to be renounced and replaced with words of blessing.

Perhaps the best place to begin is by asking our children themselves what words we've spoken that have injured them. Because the offender always has a shorter memory than the offended, we may be surprised at what they say. But it's critical to give our children genuine freedom to talk about this; if we meet their observations immediately with defensiveness or anger, we won't get any further toward solving the problem. They'll just shut down.

Once we know how we've offended, we must ask immediately and sincerely for forgiveness from our children. Even if our words weren't spoken with negative intent or were misunderstood, the offense is still real. We may try to explain what we really meant, but the bottom line is that we must still say, "I'm sorry that I hurt you with my words. Will you please forgive me?"

Keep in mind that to be sincere means we can't say something like, "*If* I've done anything wrong, please forgive me." That's not an admission of wrongdoing; it's an underhanded assertion of innocence.

Once we've asked forgiveness, we need then and there to pray with our children so that in their presence we can ask for God's forgiveness as well. Finally, we should go on to pray a blessing on them—if possible, one that specifically counteracts the curse we've just renounced.

For example, if we had said, "Can't you ever do anything right?" we can pray, "I thank You, Father, for all the things that Melissa does right. (You can even name a few in particular.) I thank You that she will be a great success in Your eyes. Please prosper and bless her now with strength and wisdom in all the things she attempts to do. In the name of the Father, and of the Son, and of the Holy Spirit, Amen."

Follow these guidelines sincerely, and I have no doubt that you'll see a change in both you and your child. Such is the power of the spoken word—to break the rule of evil, to heal, to forgive, and to bless.

May the God of peace, who through the blood of the eternal covenant brought back from the dead our Lord Jesus, that great Shepherd of the sheep, equip you with everything good for doing his will,

and may he work in us what is pleasing to him, through Jesus Christ, to whom be glory forever and ever. Amen.

Hebrews 13:21–22, KJV

11

◇

You Can't Saw Sawdust

"Let bygones be bygones." "No use crying over spilled milk." "What's done is done." "You can't turn back the clock." "Don't live in the past."

These are just a few of the clichés we tell ourselves for comfort when we think of all the things we wish we had done differently in life, or not done at all. And they all contain sound advice. Even the apostle Paul dealt this way with his past: "But one thing I do," he wrote. "Forgetting what is behind . . ." (Philippians 3:13, NIV). He didn't sit around mourning what he had done in the days before his conversion.

Nevertheless, Paul did more about his past than just put it behind him. He also used it as an inspiration for the future. He learned from his experiences, both good and bad, success and failure. So he went on to affirm: "I press on. . . ."

In light of Paul's words, take another look at the sayings we just quoted. Though each attempts to encourage, none really succeeds; they all stop short of what Paul said. Unlike Paul's statement, they fail to offer any hope for the future. Bygones really *are* bygones. What's done *is* done. And maybe you don't have to cry over spilled milk—but whether you cry or not, you still have to wipe it up.

Perhaps you've felt a bit guilty or remorseful as you've read this book because you didn't bless your kids when they were young, and now they're not living at home anymore. Maybe you feel as if you "blew" it, not just in blessing your kids, but in your parenting role in general. Or you might even be feeling a bit wistful about your own childhood and your relationship to your parents, because you know that as a child you didn't receive the blessing yourself.

If any of these things are true in your case, you may have been telling yourself, "Oh, well, no use cryin' over spilled milk. It's too late. Nothing I can do now."

That's not at all true. Actually, there's a great deal more you can do, even now. That's why I like another expression better than all the ones we mentioned. Some folks say, "You can't saw sawdust." Maybe not, but there's plenty you can make out of it.

Making Particle Board of the Past

For years lumber mills had few uses for all the sawdust they were creating when they cut up their logs. Some of it was carried off for the ignoble job of soaking up grease on the floors of butcher shops. But most of it just went to waste.

Then researchers discovered that by mixing the sawdust with resin and compressing it, they could make a product that was stronger and less expensive than the original article. Particle board was born. As a result, sawdust is now being used extensively in all types of construction today.

A similar invention rescues waste scraps of leather. I've learned about the process in my work with Bible publishers.

Did you know that there are no fewer than fifty different materials used in Bible covers? We cover the Word with pigskin, sheepskin, cowhide, and calfhide; durabond, leatherflex, skivertex, and kivar; chevo, croupon, rexine, and roncote, to name just a few. But far and away the most popular deluxe binding for Bibles is called "bonded leather."

This material is made up of all the leftover scraps of genuine leather used in other Bible covers, "reprocessed" and mixed with special resins. The result is a versatile new material that has all the qualities of the original leather, but at a lower cost.

When you think of your past as a child or as a parent, think about that particle board or the bonded leather. Have you considered how you might be able to make something new out of what's left over?

Perhaps you feel that the opportunity to be blessed by your parents or to bless your own children has passed you by, and that there's nothing you can do to go back in time and change it all. As a youngster you may have been a model child, or a rebel who turned your folks' hair solid gray. As a parent you may have used the time wisely when your kids were young to shape their character and values, or you may have "blown" it completely. You may have just sailed through your child-hood or your parenthood, blissfully unaware of all that could have been different, happy as a clam at high tide just to have survived.

In one sense, it really doesn't matter now how it all went. It's done. You're grown and out of your parents' home. Or your kids are grown and out of your home. You can't change what has happened—but you *can* change the ongoing *effects* of what happened. You can't saw sawdust, but you can make something of great value and usefulness out of it.

A Sawdust Masterpiece

A few years ago, I admired a beautiful work of art by Mario Fernandez. It was the bust of a bald eagle called "In God We Trust," and was on the mantel in the home of my sister-in-law and her husband, John and Joni Peterson.

John told me the story of the artist, a Cuban refugee who came to America with nothing more than the clothes on his back and the American dream. While still in his native land, Mario had spent two years in prison because he was a young political dissenter. So for him, the American dream repre-sented everything that couldn't possibly be realized in Cuba. But he had only been able to fulfill that dream through a strong faith in God. That's why he had named this sculpture "In God We Trust."

Soon after I admired Mario's eagle, Mary and I received one as a gift from John and Joni. When I read what this gorgeous, hand-painted, limited edition bust of the bald eagle was made from, I was completely surprised. It was made from sawdust—sawdust mixed with resin, and given value by the skill of an artist.

As I reflected on the nature of particle board, bonded leather, and Mario's masterpiece, I began to see parallels between them and the possibilities of our own lives. It seems to me that in all four cases, three things are necessary to create something new from the scraps of the old:

1. An awareness of the *value of the old, leftover scraps,* no matter what their condition.

2. A *resin* to hold the material together.

3. A *vision in the creator* of what those scraps can become, whether the new creation is particle board, bonded leather, a work of art, or a new relationship with our parents or children.

No matter what your past relationship with your parents or children has been, you can start with a clean slate today. Even if there was abuse, neglect, hypocrisy, or any number of destructive forms of behavior, those things are sawdust now, and it's up to you what you'll do with that sawdust. You can sweep it up and throw it out, saying, "Good riddance!" or you can say, "Look at this mess! What can I make out of this?"

God is the Master Artist who can look at those old leftover scraps and see the finished product as a work of art, a new creation of precious value. And God desires to take these "scraps" from our lives and mix them thoroughly with His "resin" until every piece is immersed in it. Then He can begin the process of shaping them into works of art that bring glory and praise to Him.

What's the "resin" God uses to create something new? It's His Holy Spirit. As He fills us with His Spirit and we submit to His will, He's able to knead us until we're one with His Spirit and ready for His handiwork to be completed in our lives. This process brings healing to all the wounds caused by our parents' efforts or our own efforts to shape the original material.

A Father's Final Blessing

In an earlier chapter, I spoke of my friend Paul Thigpen, who blesses his children every night. Paul's story of how he came to receive his own father's blessing, even after Paul had become an adult, wonderfully illustrates the truth that God can make a work of art out of sawdust.

Paul's dad, Travis, had grown up in a difficult situation. Travis's father loved his children, but he was an alcoholic with a violent temper. Travis was the oldest of five children who had to work long hours even as a child to contribute to the family income. What the Depression didn't take from the family, the bottle did.

It's no surprise, then, that Travis's troubled relationship with his father should become the model for his relationship with his own sons. Because of what he saw it do to his dad, Travis never touched alcohol, and for that, Paul was deeply grateful. But Paul grew up with a deeply broken relationship with Travis, whose demeanor with his children was distant and harsh.

Travis was rarely at home and had no time for play—he spent all his waking hours working hard to support another set of five kids, this time his own. Paul never remembers during those years a single time when his dad said to him, "I love you," nor when he touched him for any reason other than to administer discipline.

The near-inevitable rebellion in Paul's life took the form of an intellectual revolt against his parents' ways of thinking. At the age of twelve he declared himself an atheist, and for the following six years he remained adamantly opposed to established religion. Meanwhile, his relationship to Travis deteriorated. Even though they were spending more time together because Paul was working in the family business, Paul resented the long hours there, often feeling that he was required to work, not because he was needed, but because Travis had been required to do the same as a teenager.

By the time of Paul's graduation from high school, most folks probably would have concluded that the only thing left of his relationship with his dad was "sawdust," and that the sooner he got away from home, the better. But it was only weeks later when the Master Artist began to reveal His plans for something Paul had never dreamed would be possible.

Through a long series of events too complicated to tell here, Paul became a Christian. He had been accepted at Yale—the fulfillment of a lifelong dream—so he proceeded with his plans for a pre-law major there, even though his conversion had suddenly overturned all his values and priorities. But within months Paul heard God saying clearly, "I want you to leave school and go to the mission field." So at the end of his first semester, Paul dropped out.

If Paul's relationship with Travis was broken before, it was shattered now. Travis wasn't walking with the Lord at the time, so he found it impossible to understand how God could talk to someone—to say nothing of telling a person to pass up an Ivy League opportunity. Yale had been part of his dream as well, and he was furious.

Paul soon went to work with Continental Teen Challenge, an urban youth ministry serving in Europe. The break with his dad seemed complete. But while on the field Paul had excellent counsel from a Christian couple who recognized the need for a healing in his family relationships. They helped him to see that he himself had to take the initiative to ask Travis's forgiveness for his rebellion and bitterness. So eight months after he began work in Europe, he went home for a Christmas visit and to be reconciled with his dad.

Meanwhile, God was working on Travis, too. He noticed Paul's new attitude right away, commenting the second day he was home: "For the first time I can remember, I feel as if you're really listening to me." So by the time Paul talked with his parents and asked their forgiveness, the way was paved for a new beginning. Over the next year, through a series of crises that brought Travis to admit his need for God's help, he returned to the Lord as well.

When Paul returned to the States a year later, he had the joy of watching each of his family members receive baptism as a sign of their new life with the Lord. He decided to live at home until he went back to Yale so that he could work on his relationship with his dad. It wasn't easy. But in the following months, and then again on holidays and summer vacations, he saw a new and miraculous friendship develop.

In time, Travis became Paul's best friend. They discovered how much they had in common—things like a love for thunderstorms, grits and gravy, and old hymns. Every time they met, they embraced and said, "I love you." And Travis was the undisputed choice for best man at Paul's wedding.

You can imagine, then, the shock when Paul's family discovered only months after the wedding that Travis had inoperable lung cancer. As his father grew increasingly weaker, Paul and his wife decided to sell their home in Florida and move into his parents' home in Georgia so she could help with medical care and Paul could take his dad's place in the family business.

The last months of Travis's life were precious to Paul; because they were under the same roof again, they could talk often, and Paul could sing his father's favorite old hymns while Travis lay in bed. In the midst of their grief, God granted bright moments of joy as He was putting the finishing touches on this masterpiece of a relationship—created from sawdust. But He had one more beautiful stroke to paint to complete the work.

One day Paul was reading the biblical story of how Jacob blessed his sons on his deathbed. Suddenly he stopped and thought, *I want my father's blessing, too.* He had never heard of anyone else doing it, but that didn't matter. He wasn't going to let Travis go without granting him his blessing.

Paul took the Bible to his dad's bedside, where his father lay weak and emaciated. Paul read aloud part of the passage about Jacob, and then asked his father to give him his blessing. Travis was a little uncertain about how to proceed, but he gathered up his strength, laid his hands on Paul's head as Paul knelt by the bed, and began to pray.

What poured forth from his lips was both poetry and prophecy. Through the tears, Paul could hear him pray a number of blessings on him, but two of them meant the most: that Paul's ministry would go out to the ends of the earth, and that he would reach up to touch the face of God.

Only a few weeks later, Paul held his mother close as they watched his father die. Then Paul reached over and closed his father's eyes, saying one last time the words his dad had grown to love: "I love you." The grief was overwhelming, but the masterpiece was complete.

Only months later Paul joined the staff of a Christian magazine, beginning his career in publishing. Within a short time his ministry was going out "to the ends of the earth" through the printed word, and Travis's prophetic family blessing had been fulfilled.

Meanwhile, whenever Paul is in prayer, the other part of that blessing—that he would reach up to touch the face of God—finds its fulfillment much more easily because of what God did in his relationship to Travis. Because of their sawdust masterpiece, when Paul talks to his heavenly Father, the Face he sees reflects a familiar love, a love modeled to him by his earthly dad.

It's Never Too Late

From Paul's story you can see that it's never too late to seek your parents' blessing or to give the blessing to your adult children. If you've never asked for your parents' blessing or never given one to your own children before, start today.

You may need to clear away a mound of garbage first—some things your parents dropped on you or you dropped on your children a long time ago, but no one ever bothered to pick up. If so, pick it up now. Go back to those parents or those kids and make it right. Ask them to forgive you for all the times you messed up with them. Be specific. You know what those areas are that keep you from the kind of relationship you want with them.

Today in the United States, fifty percent of our marriages are ending in divorce, so that a staggering number of households are headed by single parents. Deep emotional wounds are being inflicted on both parents and their children. But these hurts and wounds can be healed. The resentment can be replaced by an attitude reflecting God's character to both the children and the spouse. The heart of bitterness that destroys a life can become a heart of praise and gratefulness to God.

Begin with Unilateral Forgiveness

You may feel that things are beyond saving. You might be thinking, *I really would like to do what you say, Rolf, but I know my kids (or my parents) wouldn't receive it. I know my spouse would laugh at me.* Yet I sincerely doubt that anyone would laugh at you, especially if you have truly forgiven them in your own heart before you expect them to forgive you in return.

In any case, once you've sought and granted forgiveness, their response to you is not the most important thing. You cannot control their response. You can only control your own.

The most important part for you is to know categorically that God has forgiven you, and that you need only to draw on that forgiveness. Then you must also forgive yourself. As you walk in the light of that forgiveness, you'll radiate it to those around you. When they see it, they'll be drawn to it. And at that point they can receive your forgiveness and begin to be made whole as well.

In 1974 when Mary and I were still in Puerto Rico, I was asked by my pastor to be one of seven laymen to speak at the Good Friday service in our church. He said that each of us would have five minutes to speak on one of the "seven last words" of Christ on the cross (see Matthew 27:26; Luke 23:34, 43, 46; John 19:26–30). When I asked him which of the seven words I was to speak on, he said, "You can take your pick. You're the first person I've asked." I scanned the list and selected the passage from Luke 23:34 (KJV): "Father, forgive them; for they know not what they do."

I had about two weeks' notice, more than enough time to prepare for a five-minute talk. *Anyone can talk on forgiveness for five minutes,* I reasoned, so I didn't bother to think about it until the night before I was to speak. As I sat at my desk to scratch out a brief outline for the talk, nothing came.

I sat there for several hours reading and rereading the story of the Crucifixion and commentaries on the subject. It was as though my mind had a lid on it. Nothing was coming clear, and I finally gave it a rest.

Early the next morning, I returned to my office looking for some clarity in my thoughts. Nothing. I went to church early, thinking that maybe the surroundings and music might help. (I was getting desperate by then.) Finally, I looked at the bulletin, hoping to see my name at the bottom of the list so I could gain some insight from the other speakers.

Much to my chagrin, I was first on the program. I wondered, *Why am I first? Is it because he asked me first?* And then I saw it! I was first on the program because "Father, forgive them, for they know not what they do" was the first thing Jesus said from the cross. Before He said, "My God, my God, why hast thou forsaken me?" He declared to all around Him—persecutors, friends, families, the curious—"Father, forgive them; they don't know what they're doing."

When I realized that Jesus' first concern was the unilateral forgiveness of those who were abusing Him, I couldn't wait to speak. No way was five minutes enough to share what I had just discovered.

By His example, Jesus showed us what He will do in and through us when we give Him the opportunity. The same Spirit that not only allowed Jesus to exhibit this forgiveness, but also raised Him from the dead, is the very Spirit that God wants to fill us with so we can be conformed to His likeness. Then, and only then, can we truly know the power of forgiveness to set us and our offenders free from our past.

Experiencing God's forgiveness liberates us to begin to bless our families instead of cursing them. It opens the door to speak honestly to them without shame or guilt, because Jesus bore our shame and guilt on the cross.

If you're an adult who has never been blessed by your parents, go to them and request it as Paul Thigpen did. It will liberate both you and them to experience a new level of love and acceptance. If you're a parent of grown children, go to them and clear up the past. Then ask them to let you bless them. As you do, God will bless you all.

May our Lord Jesus Christ himself and God our Father, who loved us and by his grace gave us eternal encouragement and good hope, encourage your hearts and strengthen you in every good deed and word.

May the Lord direct your hearts into God's love and Christ's perseverance.

Now may the Lord of peace himself give you peace at all times and in every way.

The Lord be with all of you.

2 Thessalonians 2:16, 17; 3:16, NIV

12

◇

Grandparents, Godparents, and Other Supplementary Parents

In our chapter called "Feedback from the Kids," Kristi Lenning mentioned that as a child, when she had friends over to spend the night, she insisted that her parents give them the blessing, too. And why not? No doubt few if any of those little visitors ever got such a blessing at home.

In fact, what *about* all those "OPKs" out there? ("OPKs," of course, are "Other People's Kids.") Who will bless them? Someone has wisely said that we may be the only Bible some people ever read. In the same way, we may be the only one ever to speak a blessing on some people. Do we dare pass up the opportunity?

Blessing children as we have defined it in this book is obviously not limited to our own children. In fact, it's not even limited to children. It extends to include the entire "human family."

Jesus' own example was one of blessing other people's kids. I believe that the event Mark's gospel tells us about (10:16) when "Jesus took the children in his arms, placed his hands on them and blessed them" was typical of the Lord. No doubt He was often surrounded by kids—not only because they felt comfortable being near Him, but also because they knew He had a blessing in store for them.

Grandparents Can Bless

The most obvious folks who are in a position to bless children other than their own are grandparents. Not only will they probably have frequent opportunities to bless their children's children; they'll have the chance to bless them within the context of a committed family relationship (aunts and uncles fall in this class, too).

My grandfather was a classic example of the blesser. He had to have loved kids: He had fourteen of them, and they gave him twenty-eight grandchildren. We always loved to be around him.

And no wonder. He was continually doing something to make us laugh. And best of all, when all the kids were together in the living room, Grandpa would sooner or later reach in his pocket, jingle his change, and start tossing nickels, dimes, and quarters on the carpet. We would all dive into a pile of bodies to be sure to get our share. It was a kind and loving gesture to show his delight in the little ones around him—his version of the "blessing." It let each child know that they had Grandpa's approval, and that was important to them.

My dad didn't carry coins for his grandchildren; instead he always had in his shirt pocket what the kids knew as "kokky"— broken pieces of hard candy. Long before his grandkids could walk or talk, they all knew that Grandpa had "kokky," where to find it, and that there was an unlimited supply of it. All they had to do was crawl up on his lap and dig in. It was his form of the "blessing."

Grandparents are extremely important in the development of character and self-esteem in a child. Some studies suggest that children who have been reared in close proximity to their grandparents and who see them often have a greater sense of security and well-being than those who don't have that privilege.

Recently I heard of a program in Minneapolis to get grandparents involved in the lives of the children of single mothers. Research by the group sponsoring this program concurred with other studies about the tremendous value of a grandfather in the life of a young boy raised in a fatherless home. This was especially evident for boys ten to fifteen years old.

If just the physical presence and social involvement of a grandparent can impact the lives of children in these situations, think of the good that's done when that grandparent actively blesses those children. That blessing can include both the verbal, hands-on-the-head, straight-out-of-Numbers 6:24–26 blessing as well as other simple kinds of blessing: the spoken words "God bless you," a loving caress, a kind word, an encouraging smile, an understanding nod, a listening ear, a forgiving kiss, a comforting shoulder. All these are accepting and approving signs of interest in the child.

Special Qualities of Grandparents

Grandparents often have one commodity that parents only have in short supply: time. So it's wonderful when they choose to invest that precious commodity in their grandchildren.

In addition, grandparents typically seem to have certain character qualities children love that their parents may not have yet developed. Many of these qualities simply come with experience—like the quality of patience.

My grandmother on my mother's side had a rare quality that was a great blessing for youngsters to be around. You could call it patience or even peacefulness, but perhaps the best word for it was serenity. She had the ability to take whatever life brought her with grace, to praise God in both the good and bad times, to remain faithful during times of intense struggle, and to serve others cheerfully without complaining, even when their needs might not be as great as her own. I don't use the word "saint" very often, but she certainly earned the title if anyone ever did.

"Gramma," as we called her, came over from Norway as a teenager and settled in Superior, Wisconsin. It was there that she married Lars Roholt, my grandfather, and gave birth to her first seven children at home over a space of ten years. During one four-year stretch of terrible grief, the first, fourth, and sixth-born children (all boys) died—one of scarlet fever at age six, one of typhoid fever at age three, and the last of dehydration at the age of six months. In addition, each of the other four children at that time also nearly died of scarlet fever.

When the sixth child was born, Gramma was so severely crippled with a form of arthritis that she could not comb her own hair for the pain, and had to crawl to climb stairs. Yet no one ever heard her complain of her lot. She gave her grief to God, who carried it for her.

Gramma's way of gaining release was to sing. She sang to God, and she sang constantly. When her heart was heavy, she sang songs in a minor key. When she had "prayed through" and her grief or concern had passed, she changed to a major key.

Gramma's arthritis improved significantly when she and her family moved away from the cold and damp conditions around Lake Superior. Soon she became a leader in her church, encouraging others to "do the work of Christ," and she was a blessing to everyone she met through her life. She also gave birth to seven more children, this time all in hospitals!

By the time she was in her early fifties, Gramma's arthritis returned, and for the remaining forty-some-odd years of her life, she was in continual pain. Yet the most negative remark I ever heard her say regarding her pain was that it kept her from doing more for others. She said, in her thick Norwegian accent, "If I yust had two good legs, I vould run and yump like a spring shicken."

One day when Gramma was ninety-two years old and living with my parents, she hobbled out from her bedroom on her walker and said to my mother, "Ya, Blanche. You know, I vas reading in dis magazine and I found a vord dat tells yust da type of person dat I am." My mother found the word Gramma had discovered. It was "optimist."

She was that all right, but she was much more. She was an "overcomer," one who considered the needs of others greater than her own (as overwhelming as hers were), and one who was always looking for ways to share the victory she knew so well in

Jesus with another who needed it. She was in every way a "blesser."

If you're a grandparent, you have a multitude of opportunities to bless your grandchildren. Keep in mind that your role in their lives is vital, and that you may have the time and the character qualities no one else can share with them just now. So make the most of it.

Godparents Can Bless, Too

Designating godparents for a child is a custom in many churches. They're chosen by the parents of a child to accompany them to the altar in their church to witness the child's baptism or dedication to the Lord. But that's just the beginning.

Traditionally, the full role of the godparents has included assuming responsibility along with the parents for the child's faith, praying for the child, encouraging the child, and blessing the child. For that reason, the selection of godparents must be a careful decision based on their Christian commitment, their willingness to take an active part in the child's spiritual development, and their closeness to the family. Sadly enough, however, all too often today the responsibility of godparents beyond standing at the side of the family during the child's dedication or baptism is not taken as seriously as it once was.

Both Mary and I are blessed with godparents who have faithfully carried out their duties to bless us, pray for us, encourage us, and—in a multitude of other ways—show us the heart of God. Hal and Helen Strand were Mary's godparents. They have prayed for her every day of her life.

When she graduated from high school, they chose an especially meaningful way to bless her. They found a scripture verse to give her for facing the future: "I will instruct thee and teach thee in the way which thou shalt go: I will guide thee with mine eye" (Psalm 32:8, KJV). Their thoughtfulness in finding this special verse for her let her know that they loved and cared about her, and that she was not alone in the decisions that lay ahead.

My godparents were my Aunt Clara and Uncle Bob. When I was just a wee young thing, Aunt Clara carried me while she and Uncle Bob accompanied my parents down the aisle, then held me while I was presented to the Lord. Although I don't remember that occasion, I clearly remember the countless times they've blessed my life since then.

Like Mary's godparents did for her, Uncle Bob and Aunt Clara have prayed for me every day of my life. The mere knowledge of this gift overwhelms me. The commitment of someone other than your own parents to pray for you daily is the highest sign of value one person can place on another. I haven't taken these prayers for granted—I've counted on them. The blessings on my life given by these precious people will last for all eternity.

If you have an opportunity to be a godparent, be sure to think through the responsibility you're taking on. If you find that you're ready to accept that challenge, then you'll have a unique opportunity to be a lifelong blessing to that godchild.

Supplementary Parents

A supplement, says Webster, is "something added to make up for a lack or deficiency." So a supplemental parent is any person who adds something to a child's life that's lacking or deficient in what has been received from his or her own parents.

No one parent, nor even two parents, can meet all the needs of a child all the time. We'll come up short somewhere. Will Rogers once said, "Everybody is ignorant, only in different subjects." So what we must do when we can't fill the bill is to find someone who can.

The need to be blessed with a parent's regular attention, approval, and good will is a real need for kids, and it's a need that's not being filled by most parents consistently. As long as the need exists and the deficiency continues, young people will keep looking for the blessing in some form or another—even if they don't realize it—until they can find someone who *will* provide it. Otherwise, they'll despair.

This is especially true with teenagers who have not yet found someone to bless them. Is it any wonder that 73 percent of the teens interviewed for *Teenage Magazine* in November 1987 said they've contemplated suicide? This same magazine noted in January 1988 that 90 percent of suicidal teens feel that their families do not understand them. The most important question in their lives is, "Does anybody care?"

Enter the volunteer supplementary parent. Psychiatrists refer to these people as "surrogate" parents, substitute authority figures who replace the father or mother in a person's feelings. The lives of these people may intersect that of the child in a variety of ways.

The danger of this situation is that as these teens and younger children go looking for a caring figure to fill the hole in their lives, many end up being emotionally, sexually, and physically abused. Our society appears to have no shortage of selfishly motivated individuals just waiting out there to take advantage of a blessing-starved kid.

As caring adult Christians, then, we need to become "blessing activists." We need to be looking for those to whom we can give a thoughtful, encouraging word. The world is full of people who are ready to receive a sincere, loving compliment, a word to brighten their day; who are anxious to have someone place value on them, to show them that they care.

But sadly, we tend to carry the same "I'm too busy right now" attitude that we communicate to our own kids over into our attitude toward the community as well. It's easier to write a check (especially a tax-deductible one) to enable someone else to "deal with those people" than it is to help them ourselves.

Even so, if we think about it, we'll realize that it doesn't really take much time to pass out a blessing or two on a daily basis. Just consider the places you go and the things you do where you usually encounter an approval-hungry kid. How simple would it be to give that child a blessing? Share the concern with your friends. Pray about it, asking God to show you what you can do to start blessing those "OPKs."

A *Church Nursery Blessing*

You can even start in church. My local congregation recently started a practice of having a husband-and-wife team head up the nursery on Sunday mornings. The couple who accepted this duty are also parents of one of the children. I was immediately in favor of the idea, as all too often there's no father figure present in the nursery.

On the day the couple's new responsibilities had been announced, I shared with them a little about our practice of blessing our children and noted that they might want to try doing it in the nursery. "Would it work," I suggested to the husband, "for you, during the hour or so you're in the nursery, to make a systematic effort each week to pick up the infants individually, hold them in your arms, place your hand on their head, and bless them?" The couple was interested and eager to hear more.

This practice may only be a once-a-week experience for those little babies, but at least it's that much. In addition, for the couple in charge of the nursery it could establish a lifelong practice in their own home with their little daughter that could some day spread to other children as well.

Blessing Other Adults

The biblical act of blessing was not limited to blessing children; people of *every* age need to receive the favor and power of God. In a sense, each of us has a child still inside, and if that child was never blessed by its parents, it's still looking for the blessing. The search doesn't end when we turn twenty-one.

The person who needs a blessing may be as close to us as our own brother or sister. I have a friend who grew up in a home without the blessing, but who has since been blessed as an adult by caring Christian pastors and friends. When he sought for a way to bless his youngest sister, who also grew up without the blessing, the Lord provided a unique opportunity: His sister became engaged, and she asked him to "give her away" at the wedding (their father had died).

In preparation for the event, my friend wrote a song called "The Blessing," tailor-made for the situation. When the point came in the ceremony to answer the question, "Who gives this woman in marriage?" the song was his reply.

The words he sang first affirmed their own cherished relationship, and how even when they were young, he had taken a fatherly role with her, teaching her nursery rhymes and singing her lullabies. Then the lyrics spoke of their father's love for her, of the blessing he would surely have given if he could have been present for the occasion, and of the blessing that her older brother in her father's place now bestowed on her and her new husband. The last verse summed up the song's prayer of blessing:

> *Long life and fruitfulness,*
> *courage and faithfulness,*
> *cover your dwelling place*
> *and evermore remain.*
> *God's joy, your waking cry;*
> *God's peace, your lullaby;*
> *God's love, your melody,*
> *and yours, His refrain.* [1]

When the song was done there were no dry eyes in the congregation. For the moment, my friend had become his little sister's supplementary parent, and he had received the privilege of speaking to her a blessing that would last a lifetime.

Blessing a Co-worker

In addition to the grown members of our own family, most of us have a number of close contacts with other adults whose ongoing relationships with us could provide the context for speaking a blessing. Our co-workers on the job are one possibility for such a ministry.

This reality was confirmed for me one day when I was talking with a co-worker about the blessing. She said, "You know, Rolf, I've never in my entire life been blessed by anyone."

"Well, then," I replied, "we need to change that right now." So then and there I laid my hands on her head and spoke to her the blessing I spoke every night to my children.

By the time I was done, she was weeping. The power of those simple words had moved her deeply and ministered God's love to her right on the spot.

Whether children or adults, countless people are waiting out there for someone to speak God's blessing into their lives. Those of us who are grandparents or godparents already have a clearly defined area of responsibility and opportunity with a particular child or children. But even for those without grandchildren or godchildren, the possibilities for blessing are limitless—if you start today.

Now to Him who is able to keep you from stumbling, and to make you stand in the presence of His glory blameless with great joy, to the only God our Savior, through Jesus Christ our Lord, be glory, majesty, dominion and authority, before all time and now and forever. Amen.

Jude 1:24–25

13

◇

The Blessing As a Way of Life

Everybody loved my father—everybody, that is, except Mr. and Mrs. Aune. They were our neighbors on the lake in Wisconsin where we lived for thirteen years. It wasn't a personal thing, mind you. At least it didn't start out that way.

Twenty years before we moved into the house next to theirs, the Aunes had a severe crossing of wills with a member of their church. Rather than resolve that conflict and move on in their faith, they became extremely bitter, and not just toward that other member or even the entire membership of their church. No, they were bitter toward anyone who went to any church anywhere. And they let it be known often.

The Aunes were in their mid-sixties when we met them. When they first heard that we were Christians, they wanted nothing to do with us, or at least with our faith. We tried to honor their wishes and stayed to ourselves as much as possible. But God arranged circumstances otherwise.

We had a dog, half collie and half German shepherd, named "Shultz." Our home was in the country on several acres of land, and Shultz had ample room to run; but somehow it was never quite enough, so he made free use of the Aunes' yard, too.

Mrs. Aune was especially bothered by Shultz's trespassing and showed it by shouting all kinds of things at him that he didn't understand. She even had the town constable call on us once about him. We really did try to keep Shultz at home, but when a boat pulling a water skier would come close to our shoreline, a ball and chain wouldn't have kept him home.

One day Mrs. Aune and Shultz had a showdown. She was out in her yard digging dandelions from the lawn, using a picker with a five-foot wooden handle on one end and a sharp, twin-pointed blade on the other. When Shultz chased through her yard, she wound up like a softball pitcher and let the lethal weapon fly. Fortunately for Shultz, she was out of practice and the lance sailed harmlessly about six inches over his back.

Within minutes, though, someone was pounding on our door. Having observed the incident with the dandelion picker through our windows, we knew who was there, so Dad offered to answer the knock.

What happened next I'll never forget. I was scared for my dad as he opened the door. There was Mrs. Aune, literally bouncing up and down on our porch with rage, like some plastic wind-up toy.

For what seemed like forever, Mrs. Aune assailed my dad at the top of her lungs. When she had nothing more to say, she just stood there sputtering like an old motor. Finally, she ran out of gas and stopped. Then Dad looked at her, and with his heart overflowing with compassion, he said, "My dear Mrs. Aune, I am so sorry that we have upset you so. Will you ever forgive us? We'll try not to let it happen again. God bless you, Mrs. Aune." She was defenseless. For a brief moment, she stood there in stunned silence. Then she spun on her heels and charged back to her home, hunched over under the weight of the "coals of fire" my dad had lovingly placed on her.

We didn't see either Mr. and Mrs. Aune for several weeks after that, and Dad became concerned about them. Their lawn, normally kept nicely mowed, was overgrown and in desperate need of cutting. So after considerable prodding from him, my brother Kent and I were finally convinced to go over and mow their lawn. We were about fourteen and sixteen years old at the time, and quite honestly, this wasn't how we had planned to spend that warm summer day at the lake. It was an all-day job mowing and raking their large lawn. But to honor Dad's wishes, we did it, however reluctantly.

No sign of life appeared in the Aune house while we did

our work, but we knew they were home. Then two weeks later, Kent and I protested again as Dad asked us to mow their lawn once more. This time we saw Mrs. Aune peeking from behind the curtains as we mowed, but she still didn't come out.

Two more weeks went by when Dad looked over at the Aune's lawn and said, "Well, boys?" We knew what he wanted and went one more time to mow their grass. This time Mrs. Aune came outside just as we were finishing the yard, and she brought a tray with a large glass of lemonade for each of us. She thanked us for mowing her lawn and explained that her husband, Al, had not been well. We told her we were sorry her husband was ill and that we were glad to help in the yard in any way we could until he got well.

Later that fall, my folks received a phone call from Mrs. Aune. "Can you come quickly? Al is very ill." Mom and Dad rushed over to their home and entered it for the first time. Mrs. Aune took them into the bedroom where her husband lay. They talked with Mr. Aune about his sickness, his past with the church, the state of his soul, and the redeeming blood of Christ that could make him clean again. Mr. Aune listened, thanked them for coming, and asked them to please come back.

Over the next few weeks, Dad and Mom visited the Aunes in their home several times. Finally, the day came when both Mr. and Mrs. Aune prayed to receive Christ as their Savior. I can still remember the tears of joy in my parents' eyes when they told us what had happened.

Just two weeks later, Mr. Aune went to be with the Lord. Mrs. Aune joined our church and soaked up everything she could. The following summer she was baptized in Lake Wissota, along with a number of others from that church. She grew in her faith and became a close friend of our family. Then a few years later, she joined her husband in the presence of the Lord.

What would have happened to Mr. and Mrs. Aune if my dad had answered her back in a harsh way that summer afternoon? Instead, God used a soft answer, a kind word, a loving deed—in short, a blessing—to expand His kingdom here on earth.

A Way of Life

Dad's response to Mrs. Aune that day was not an isolated instance of Christlikeness. You see, much of what I've learned about blessing I learned from my father. He was more than a man who knew how to bless people. He was a man who knew the blessing as a way of life.

The biblical portrait of King David shows us another man who knew the blessing as a way of life. In fact, of the many recorded uses in the Bible of some form of the word "bless," more than seventy are attributed to David. And on one particular occasion, when he regained the ark of the Lord from his enemies, this king displayed a pattern that we might all want to imitate. At that time David spoke a blessing in three directions. We read that he blessed God for His goodness, saying: "Blessed be the Lord, the God of Israel, from everlasting to everlasting" (1 Chronicles 16:36, NASB). He also blessed all the people around him: "David finished giving burnt offerings and fellowship offerings to God. Then he used the Lord's name to bless the people" (v. 2). Finally, he gave the blessing to his family: "Then all the people left. Each person went to his own home. And David also went home to bless his family" (v. 43).

As we read the many stories about David in the Scripture, we read about someone who seems to have been continually blessing God, blessing his family, and blessing the people. His son Solomon was evidently so impressed with the example that he followed the pattern his father had established (see 1 Kings 8:12–15). No wonder, then, that King David, the man of blessing, was called a man after God's own heart, who would do everything God wanted him to do (Acts 13:22).

The Center of a Widening Circle

The main point of this book has been to encourage parents, and especially fathers, to begin an intentional and regular habit of speaking blessing to their children. We've seen the power of this blessing to transform lives, as well as the power of cursing to destroy them. We discussed ways to get started blessing our kids, ways to break the power of curses over them, and ways to let God make something new out of the old "sawdust" of our lives. And we've said that we have the privilege and responsibility to bless, not only our children, but all the people around us, and even the Lord Himself.

The family blessing spoken regularly over our kids is just the center of a circle whose circumference can widen to include all our speech in all our relationships. To begin the process of effecting that kind of transformation in our lives may seem like a daunting challenge, and it is. But the beauty of it all—and I hope this is clear now that this book must draw to a close—is that the change begins with that one small point of commitment, that one little step of establishing a family habit that takes only a few minutes, but pays benefits for a lifetime. As in so many other things, when we start by learning to be faithful in little things, we can go on to become faithful in greater things (Matthew 25:21).

Restoring the Mansion

Blessing our children and others around us is like so many other disciplines of the Christian life. It can all too easily be swept under the rug or into a corner and neglected. The problem with our "under the rug" tendency, of course, is that soon we end up with so much there, both good and bad, we don't know where to start to clean it all up. That's normal, and it happens to the best of us. But ultimately, we have to deal with what's "under the rug," and it's better to start now than to wait till later.

The devil used to tell me the lie that having garbage in my life was okay as long as I could keep it hidden from others. Several years ago I was going through a particularly difficult time spiritually. I felt as if I had so much garbage under the carpets, in the corners, and in every closet of my life that it was all starting to spill over into the public areas. When things finally got so that I couldn't stand it any more, I cried out to God for help.

He came and began a wonderful heart cleaning. It seemed as though He walked through every room of my heart, shining the gentle light of His Holy Spirit into the darkest corner of each. There was no condemnation or judgment, just the knowledge that everything was going to be fine.

I asked, "Lord, how will we ever clean this mess up?" And He answered, "Don't worry about that. We'll just take it one room at a time." Then He reminded me of the tremendous comfort in Paul's words to the Philippians: "Being confident of this very thing, that he which hath begun a good work in you will perform it until the day of Jesus Christ" (1:6, KJV).

On that particular day when God began this cleansing work, an article in the local newspaper caught my eye. It told about an old, stately mansion in St. Paul, Minnesota, that had been the pride and joy of its owners during its heyday. Through years of rough use and poor maintenance, however, the estate had fallen into disrepair. Finally, it was abandoned and slated to be demolished by the city fathers who saw no value in it.

Only days before the scheduled demolition, a young couple drove by it and, looking beyond what it was, saw what it could become. So they decided to try to buy it and restore it. An unusual agreement was reached finally between the city and the couple: The city sold them the mansion for one dollar on the condition that they move in on the day of closing. The couple agreed, and on closing day they moved in.

The house was a filthy, rat-infested, broken-windowed disaster, fit only to be destroyed—to everyone, that is, but this young couple. The renovation took nearly three years to complete, but when it was finished, it reflected the character of the new owners in every room. When the reporter who wrote the article asked them how they managed to do the job, they replied that after a walk through every room, noting what needed to be done, they decided to start by finishing one room at a time before going on to the next.

I'm deeply grateful that God in His wisdom deals that way with us. We're all still being remodeled by His Spirit. And that should give us hope for the changes we'd like to see take place in our lives and the lives of our family members.

As you've read through this book, maybe God has spoken to you by His Spirit. Maybe He's pointed out some lumps in your carpet and said, "You know, that really doesn't belong there. Let me help you clean it up."

If He has, now's the time to let Him start the cleaning job. Just as the old, condemned mansion reflected the character of the couple who bought it and remodeled it, let God begin to reflect His character in your life through His Spirit's remodeling efforts.

Start Where You Are

Maybe some of what you've been reading about the family blessing rings true, while other points don't relate to your experience at all. That's as it should be. It's much like going through a smörgåsbord: More than likely all the food is good, but not all of it appeals to you at the time. So just take what you can benefit from now and put it to work in your life.

Start with the most vital part. Maybe you need restoration with your parents who never blessed you. Maybe you need forgiveness from your children who are grown and gone. Maybe God is emphasizing to you the point about speaking well of others. Whatever it is, start there.

Don't worry about understanding everything before you do anything. Begin to apply the principles of blessing by starting *where you are*. It's better to apply what you do understand and make some mistakes along the way than to wait until everything is clear. The rest will become clear in time.

Meanwhile, don't be afraid of "botching things up" when you begin. Others will be supportive and eager to help. If your heart is right in what you do, God will make up the difference.

Start to bless! Start today! It carries with it rich rewards that begin to accrue immediately to all involved. The apostle Paul said: "The Lord has assigned to each his task. I planted the seed, Apollos watered it, but God made it grow . . . and each will be rewarded according to his own labor" (1 Corinthians 3:5–8, NIV). God has assigned to each of us the "task" of blessing, and He will give the reward.

A Heritage of Blessing

Perhaps the greatest reward of blessing is the heritage of blessing it allows us to leave our children. I know that kind of heritage well, because my father left one for my brothers and me.

Dad was a giant in my eyes. He loved my mother and his boys, and he showed it. He was a hard worker and a good provider. He was diligent in taking his family with him to church.

He never said hello or good-bye to us without a hug and an "I love you." He never raised his voice to my mother, nor she to him, and I never heard them argue or fight.

When I was a child, every morning as I stumbled out of my bedroom, I would see Dad lying on the couch reading his Bible and praying for his family. His one overwhelming motivation in life was to see each of his three boys come to know and love God with all their hearts.

Dad and Mom also prayed together daily. One of the things they prayed was that each of us boys would find a wife who loved us and shared our faith and commitment to the Lord. Those prayers have been wonderfully answered.

When Mary and I were married in January of 1968, we received many beautiful gifts and loving wishes. But one gift in particular that both Mary and I treasure to this day was the scripture verse my parents gave us as a lifelong blessing on our marriage: "And be ye kind one to another, tenderhearted, forgiving one another, even as God for Christ's sake hath forgiven you" (Ephesians 4:32, KJV).

Dad kept short accounts, whether it was in business or in personal relationships. One of my favorite stories he used to tell us as kids concerned the little girl in Norway who asked her mother when Jesus was coming back.

"Well," her mother told her, "we don't know when that will be. It could be any time."

The daughter thought for a moment and said, "Then, Mother, it's pretty important that we have our suitcase packed, isn't it?"

Dad's bags were always packed. His accounts were always current, and he was always ready to go.

My Dad's Last Day

On January 15, 1985, Mom and Dad rose early, well before dawn, just as they always did. Then they went to their favorite chairs to read and pray together.

After the Bible itself, Dad's favorite book was a devotional by the Norwegian author Frederick Wisloff called *Rest a While.* He had read it through countless times in both Norwegian and English. This is what he read that morning:

> "Like a weaver I have rolled up my life; He cuts me off from the loom; from day to night Thou dost bring me to an end" (Isaiah 38:12).
>
> A human life is likened unto a tapestry that is to be woven. Day by day the shuttle moves back and forth, and the tapestry grows. As thread is laid upon thread the design begins to emerge. A thread is such a tiny thing. And yet the whole tapestry is made up of such threads. If some threads are improperly woven, the whole design will be marred.
>
> A day appears so small and insignificant. And yet, each day is a part of my whole life. If each single day is lived improperly and carelessly, what will this do to the design of my life?
>
> When the tapestry is finished, it is rolled up, and the ends of the threads are cut off. Then it can be woven no more. It is put away until the day when it is placed on exhibition and judged.

Dear God, grant that the tapestry of my life may be properly woven. I give Thee the shuttle. Do with me as Thou wilt, if only Thy image may some day be the design in my tapestry when the threads of my life are cut off, and the tapestry is judged.[1]

When Dad finished reading this, he wept as he poured out his heart to his Father in prayer. I should note that Dad rarely cried—except in prayer. But when he prayed, he was often so overwhelmed by God's love for him that he would weep with gratitude. And this day he was as grateful as ever for all that God had done.

As he prayed, Dad interceded, as he always did, for his wife, his boys and their wives, his grandchildren, and his great grandson. And then he prayed for himself, that the tapestry of his life would not be marred by an improperly woven thread. He prayed that God would cleanse him of any area of sin in his life, and that he would be clean as he stood before Him.

That evening my brother, Loren, and his wife, Clairice, went to my parents' house for supper. As they sat around the table afterward, Dad said, "You know, I have been dreaming a lot lately, and it is usually the same dream. Sometimes it lasts all night. I see myself as part of a vast multitude of believers standing before the throne of God, and we are all worshiping the Lord. Sometimes I will look around at the people in the crowd, and I will recognize some of them as friends. But, you know, as I recognize them, I realize that all these friends have died. Do you think there is anything to these dreams?"

Loren and Clairice didn't quite know what to say. Two days earlier, after the Sunday morning service, Dad had given a friend a hug and said to him, "You know, Terry, I just long to be with my Lord, don't you?" So they wondered about what all this might mean.

Then, about 9:30 that evening, after a bowl of ice cream and the evening news, Dad gave Mom a tender hug, told her how much he loved her, breathed out a sigh—and was gone. Gone to be with the Lord he loved and served. He was seventy-eight.

Not a day goes by without something reminding me of Dad. A year ago, for instance, when my son was going through some times of searching and questioning his faith, I felt I should drive up to his dorm at college and take him out for some dessert. As we talked well into the night, he reminisced.

"Dad," he recalled, "four years ago when Grandpa was still alive, I stopped by to see him and Grandma. We talked for a while, and when I was about to leave, I gave them both a hug and a kiss and told them I loved them. Then Grandpa said, 'Carlton, you know, my deepest desire for you is that you know and love the Lord with all your heart.'

"You know, Dad," Carlton said, "those are the last words Grandpa ever said to me." And we both wept.

Several weeks after Dad went to be with the Lord, Mom was going through some of his belongings. Tucked away there was a letter to his three sons and our families. It was written in his own hand, and told us about his childhood in Norway, how he met our mother, and how he loved the Lord. Before he ended that letter he made certain we knew what was beating most in his heart for us:

> Now in closing I just want you to know that we love you all—children, your spouses, grandchildren, and great grandchildren. We pray for you and mention your name before the throne of grace every day. Our most sincere prayer is that we may all meet home in that glory land some day. Stay close to Jesus and He will stay close to you. Jesus says, "Fear not, for I am with you. Be not dismayed for I am your God, I will help you and strengthen you and uphold you with the right hand of my righteousness."

In these words Dad was giving us his blessing. But in a powerful sense his whole *life* was a blessing. He knew the heart of God, and the one overpowering desire of his life was that his three boys and their families would also know that same heart of God. To that end he committed his life—a commitment that my mother shared, and that she carries on with her own prayers and blessings.

A Beautiful Tapestry

What is the family blessing? It's an active commitment to our children's highest good. And what is that highest good? That they might know and love the Lord their God with all their heart.

Perhaps the story of my father's last day can help us take a step back from the hectic pace of our normal schedule and consider the big picture of our lives. Each little word, each interaction with our kids, is a thread that joins many others to form the fabric of our children's character. What will that fabric be? Each attitude we cultivate is a stitch in the tapestry of our own lives. What will be the final pattern of that tapestry when we one day present it to God for His approval and pleasure?

If we learn, as my father did, to make the blessing a way of life, our children's fabric will be strong, and the tapestry of a godly example we leave as their heritage will be beautiful. Then truly the Lord will bless us and keep us; the Lord will make His face to shine upon us and be gracious to us; the Lord will lift up His countenance upon us and give us peace. What greater blessing could we ask?

---------------- ◇ ----------------

Appendix
Some Blessings You Can Use

Biblical Blessings:

The Lord bless thee, and keep thee: The Lord make his face shine upon thee, and be gracious unto thee: The Lord lift up his countenance upon thee, and give thee peace (Number 6:23–26).

Grace to you and peace from God our Father, and the Lord Jesus Christ (Romans 1:7).

Now the God of hope fill you with all joy and peace in believing, that ye may abound in hope, through the power of the Holy Ghost . . . (Romans 15:5, 6, 13, 33).

The grace of our Lord Jesus Christ be with you. Amen (Romans 16:20).

The grace of the Lord Jesus Christ, and the love of God, and the communion of the Holy Ghost, be with you all. Amen (2 Colossians 13:14).

. . . the grace of our Lord Jesus Christ be with your spirit. Amen (Galatians 6:16, 18).

Now the Lord of peace himself give you peace always by all means. The Lord be with you all (2 Thessalonians 3:16, 18).

Now the God of peace, that brought again from the dead our Lord Jesus, that great shepherd of the sheep, through the blood of the everlasting covenant, Make you perfect in every good work to do his will, working in you that which is wellpleasing in his sight, through Jesus Christ; to whom be glory for ever and ever. Amen (Hebrews 13:20, 21, 25).

But the God of all grace, who hath called us unto his eternal glory by Christ Jesus, after that ye have suffered a while, make you perfect, stablish, strenghthen, settle you. To him be glory and dominion for ever and ever. Amen (1 Peter 5:10, 11, 14).

Grace and peace be multiplied unto you through the knowledge of God, and of Jesus our Lord, According as his divine power hath given unto us all things that pertain unto life and godliness, through the knowledge of him that hath called us to glory and virtue: Whereby are given unto us exceeding great and precious promises: that by these ye might be partakers of the divine nature, having escaped the corruption that is in the world through lust (2 Peter 1:2–4).

Grace be with you, mercy, and peace, from God the Father, and from the Lord Jesus Christ, the Son of the Father, in truth and love (2 John 3).

From the Jewish tradition:

May God be good to you
>and keep the covenant he made with Abraham, Isaac, and Jacob,
>and his faithful servants.

May he fill each of you with the desire to worship him
>and to do his will eagerly with all your heart and soul.

May he enable you to understand his law and his commands.

May he give you peace
>answer your prayers,
>forgive your sins,
>and never abandon you in times of trouble.

2 Maccabees 1:2–5, Good News Bible

Now then, give praise to the God of the universe, who has done great things everywhere, who brings us up from the time we are born, and deals with us mercifully. May he give us happiness and allow us to have peace . . . forever. May he continue his mercy to us and rescue us in our time of need.

                    adapted from Sirach 50:22–24, Good News Bible

May He who causes peace to reign in His high heavens, let peace descend on us, on all Israel, and all the world.[1]

May the One who has been gracious to you continue to favor you with all that is good.[2]

May God bless you and guide you. Be strong for the truth, charitable in your words, just and loving in your deeds. A noble heritage has been entrusted to you; guard it well.[3]

We praise You, O God, the Source of Light. Let Your light shine upon us. May our hearts and our homes be illumined by the assurance of Your love, and sanctified by the sense of Your presence.[4]

From the Catholic tradition:

May the Lord Jesus Christ be with you that he may defend you; within you that he may sustain you; before you that he may lead you; behind you that he may protect you; above you that he may bless you: he who lives and reign with the Father and the Holy Spirit for ever and ever. Amen.[5]

(For newlyweds)

May almighty God bless you by the Word of his mouth, and unite your hearts in the enduring bond of pure love.

May you be blessed in your children, and may the love that you lavish on them be returned a hundredfold.

May the peace of Christ dwell always in your hearts and in your home; may you have true friends to stand by you, both in joy and in sorrow.

May you be ready with help and consolation for all those who come to you in need; and may the blessings promised to the compassionate descend in abundance on your house.

May you be blessed in your work and enjoy its fruits.

May cares never cause you distress, nor the desire for earthly possessions lead you astray; but may your hearts' concern be always for the treasures laid up for you in the life of heaven.

May the Lord grant you fullness of years, so that you may reap the harvest of a good life, and after you have served him with loyalty in his kingdom on earth, may he take you up into his eternal dominions in heaven.

Through our Lord Jesus Christ, his Son, who lives and reigns with him in the unity of the Holy Spirit, God, for ever and ever. Amen.[6]

(For a child)
O Lord Jesus Christ, Son of the living God, begotten in eternity, you willed to be born in time. You love the innocence of childhood, and lovingly embraced and blessed the little children who were brought to you. Anticipate the needs of this child (these children) with your tender blessings, and grant that no evil may corrupt his (her, their) mind, but that, advancing in age, in wisdom, and in grace, he (she, they) may live so as to please you always. You who live and reign with God the Father in the unity of the Holy Spirit, God, for ever and ever. May the blessing of almighty God, the Father and the Son and the Holy Spirit, descend upon you and remain for ever. Amen.[7]

(For a home)
O Lord God almighty, bless this house. In it may there be health, chastity, victory over sin, strength, humility, goodness of heart and gentleness, full observance of your law and gratefulness to God, the Father, and the Son, and the Holy Spirit. And may this blessing remain upon this house and upon those who live here, now and for ever and ever. Amen.[8]

From the Presbyterian tradition:

(For newlyweds)
God the Father, God the Son, God the Holy Ghost, bless, preserve, and keep you; the Lord mercifully with his favor look upon you, and so fill you with his grace that you may live faithfully together in this life, and in the world to come may have life everlasting. Amen.[9]

From the Anglican tradition:

Watch over your child, O Lord, as his (her) days increase; bless and guide him (her) wherever he (she) may be, keeping him (her) unspotted from the world. Strengthen him (her) when he (she) stands; comfort him (her) when discouraged or sorrowful; raise him (her) up if he (she) should fall; and in his (her) heart may your peace which passes understanding abide all the days of his (her) life; through Jesus Christ our Lord. Amen.[10]

(For someone who is sick)
The Almighty Lord, who is a most strong tower to all those who put their trust in him, to whom all things in heaven, in earth, and under the earth, bow and obey: be now and evermore your defense; and make you know and feel that there is no other Name under heaven given to us, in whom and through whom you may receive health and salvation, but only the Name of our Lord Jesus Christ. Amen.[11]

God be with you till we meet again;
by His counsels guide, uphold you,
with His sheep securely fold you;
'neath His wings protecting hide you,
daily manna still provide you;
when life's perils thick confound you,
put His arms unfailing round you;
keep love's banner floating o'er you,
smite death's threatening wave before you:
God be with you till we meet again.

Jeremiah E. Rankin[12]

From the Methodist tradition:

The peace of God which passes all understanding, keep your hearts and minds in the knowledge and love of God, and of His Son, Jesus Christ our Lord; and the blessing of God Almighty, the Father, the Son, and the Holy Spirit, be among you and remain with you always. Amen.[13]

(For the nation)
Grant us peace, your most precious gift, O eternal Source of peace. Bless our country, that it may ever be a stronghold of peace, and the advocate of peace in the councils of nations. May contentment reign within its borders, health and happiness within its homes. Strengthen the bonds of friendship and fellowship between all the inhabitants of our land. Plant virtue in every soul; and may the love of your Name hallow every home and every heart. May You be praised, O Lord, Giver of peace, Amen.[14]

An Irish Blessing:

May the road rise to greet you;
may the wind be always at your back.
May the sun shine bright upon your face,
the rain fall soft upon your fields;
and until we meet again,
may God hold you in the palm of His hand.

Notes

Chapter 1

1. Larry Christenson, *The Christian Family* (Minneapolis: Bethany Fellowship, 1970). The section of this excellent book that first introduced me to the notion of the family blessing is on pages 195–197, "Presenting Your Children to God—Through Blessing."

2. Author's adaptation of the text from the King James Version.

Chapter 2

1. See Larry G. Lenning, *Blessing in Mosque and Mission* (Pasadena, California: William Carey Library, 1980), p. 74. Much of the material in this chapter was drawn from this excellent study of the notion of blessing.

Chapter 3

1. From *Fiddler on the Roof* by Jerry Bock, Sheldon Harnick and Arnold Perl. Music and lyrics copyright © 1964 by Sunbeam Music Corp. Used with permission.

Chapter 7

1. Lenning, pp. 94–95.

NOTES

Chapter 9

1. Zig Ziglar, *See You at the Top* (Gretna, Louisiana: Pelican Publishing Company, Inc., copyright 1975, 1977 by Zig Ziglar) 118, 119.

Chapter 12

1. Copyright 1990 by Paul Thigpen. Used with permission.

Chapter 13

1. Frederick Wisloff, *Rest a While.* This cherished devotional, worn out by my father in both English and Norwegian, was originally published in Norwegian in 1948 under the title, *Hvil Eder Litt,* by *Indremisjonsforlaget* A.s., Oslo, Norway.

Appendix

1. *Gates of the House: The New Union Home Prayerbook* (New York: Central Conference of American Rabbis, 1977), p. 15.
2. *Gates,* p. 22.
3. *Gates,* p. 32.
4. *Gates,* p. 41.
5. *English Ritual* (Collegeville, Minnesota: The Liturgical Press, 1964), p. 449.
6. *English Ritual,* pp. 369–370.
7. *English Ritual,* pp. 399–401.
8. *English Ritual,* pp. 457.
9. *The Book of Church Order of the Presbyterian Church in the United States* (Richmond, Virginia: Presbyterian Committee of Publication, rev. ed., 1938), p. 197.
10. Adapted from *The Book of Common Prayer* (New York: Oxford University Press, 1944), pp. 597–8.
11. Adapted from the *BCP,* p. 314.
12. *The Hymnbook* (Richmond, Virginia: Presbyterian Church in the United States, et al., 1955), p. 75.
13. Adapted from *The Methodist Hymnal* (Nashville: The Methodist Publishing Company, 1939), p. 519.
14. Adapted from *The Methodist Hymnal,* p. 517.